Our Changing World

Book 2: A Sustainable Civilization

Unraveling the Threads of Change

James Fountain

T R E E L I N E   P U B L I C A T I O N S

ISBNs:

Hardcover: 978-1-963443-04-2
Paperback: 978-1-963443-05-9
eBook: 978-1-963443-06-6
Audiobook: 978-1-963443-07-3

Acknowledgments And Dedication

Before we venture into the heart of this series, let's take a moment to acknowledge the hands and hearts that have been instrumental in bringing this work to life. It is with deep gratitude that I recognize the individuals and communities whose unwavering support and boundless inspiration have laid the cornerstone for these pages. Their contributions have not only enriched this journey but have also been pivotal in shaping the narratives that unfold within.

To start, this series stands as a testament to the guardians of wisdom through the ages—Indigenous peoples, whose very essence is woven into the Earth's rhythms, educators and seekers of knowledge who illuminate our understanding, and you, the valiant souls navigating the sustainability frontier. Your endeavors, though often stretched thin by the magnitude of your obligations and the ceaseless demands for your expertise, are the cornerstone upon which we dare to envision a future brimming with hope and harmony. In these pages lies a shared reservoir of insights, a lighthouse for those teetering on the edge of this crucial movement, aiming to cast light on the path ahead with lessons from my journey, igniting a spark within yours.

The dedication you exhibit, even when overwhelmed and overcommitted, underscores a collective resolve that transcends personal accolades. It's driven by a deep-seated desire for impact, a shared obsession with catalyzing meaningful change in the realms of sustainability, climate action, and human rights. Your commitment speaks to a profound yearning for a deeper connection with the world around us, a connection that is less about individual recognition and more about the collective soul of our planet. In an era shadowed by division, your tireless efforts weave a narrative of unity and hope, showcasing the monumental impact we can achieve through values-driven action and the pursuit of real, tangible solutions. This series seeks not only to honor your undertaking but to amplify it, offering it as a clarion call to all who dream of a tomorrow where our planet is revered, and our collective well-being is cherished.

In this vast journey, Mona, your steadfast support has been my compass, guiding me through the tumultuous and the tranquil alike. Your sacrifices, quietly monumental, from the solitary evenings while I was ensconced in thought or sequestered at the local bar, to the boundless reservoir of patience and encouragement you offered amid my sea of doubts. Our countless brainstorming sessions—naming series, books, and chapters—have been pivotal. This endeavor, imbued with your love and belief, mirrors not just my efforts but the essence of your spirit. The laughter we shared, our nocturnal dialogues, and even the moments of companionable silence have woven a rich tapestry into this work. You have been my muse, my confidante, and my untiring partner through every zenith and nadir. Your love, steadfast and grounding; your incredible life story, a wellspring of inspiration; this milestone bears witness to the enduring strength of our shared journey.

As we stand on the cusp of new adventures, I am buoyed by the knowledge that with you by my side, there are no bounds to the stories we can tell, the worlds we can explore, and the impacts we can make. Here's to the chapters yet unwritten, the tales yet untold, and the journey that continues to unfold with you, Mona, as my guiding star.

And finally, to Liam, my cherished companion whose absence has left a silence too profound for words. I miss you, buddy. In my heart, I envision you in a realm where the forest trails stretch into eternity, where mountain meadows sprawl under the open sky, where tennis balls are abundant, and marrow-filled bovine bones are yours for the taking.

Liam, you exemplified the essence of an ideal Earth citizen—your love, dedication, empathy, and compassion were lessons in themselves, showing me the heights to which we can aspire. Your soul, luminous and guiding, illuminated the path of what life should embody. Through your eyes, I learned to see the world not just as it is but as it could be, filled with love and boundless joy. This book and the series that contains it, while a dedication to the guardians of our planet and the stewards of knowledge, is also a tribute to you, Liam. Your spirit, a guiding star in the vast cosmos of our journey, continues to lead me toward love, empathy, and the profound connections that weave the fabric of life. Thank you for teaching me, for being my compass in exploring what it truly means to live fully and love unconditionally. Your legacy is etched not just in these pages but in my ambition of the being I hope to become.

-JF-

Table of Contents

Preface

n the continuum of human knowledge and the quest for a harmonious existence with our planet, few endeavors are as pivotal as understanding our role in shaping the future. The *Our Changing World* series is a literary tapestry that weaves together diverse strands of ecological thought, cultural sensitivity, and sustainable governance. It is with a sense of urgency and a deep reverence for the delicate balance of life on Earth we enter into the narrative of this second book.

At the heart of this series lies a simple truth: Our world is in a constant state of flux and the decisions we make today will echo through generations. This book seeks not only to shed light on the paths those before us tread but, more importantly, to illuminate the paths that still lie ahead. Its pages are filled with the central thoughts that must guide our hands as we shape the global ecology. We delve into the motivations behind cultural practices, explore the foundations of ethical sustainability, and investigate the fusion of environmental care into the fabric of business.

Our journey through this evolving series is akin to embarking on an expedition across a landscape teeming with both risk and opportunity. The inaugural installment, *Threads of Green*, set the stage with an examination of the sinews that bind cultural diversity and sustainability. It highlighted how intimately the health of our ecosystem is intertwined with the recognition and integration of diverse cultural insights.

As we further our exploration, the focus of this second book becomes clear. It is an in-depth examination of the ethical dimensions that must anchor our relationship with the planet—a relationship defined by care, stewardship, and respect. Through its chapters, we'll trace the origins and evolution of environmental ethics while intertwining these discourses with diverse cultural viewpoints to mobilize education, art, and storytelling as catalysts for change.

By dissecting themes of ethical consideration, innovation, and strategic cooperation, we knit together a vision of a world where sustainability is the pulsing heart of our societal endeavors. This vision underlies the book's mission to illuminate the transformative shifts in ethics, understanding, and enterprise principles that are vital to surmounting the ecological and social challenges we face.

Sustainability is not a solitary melody but a global symphony played in various rhythms and tunes. It is this symphony that offers a profound insight: While our cultures and climates may differ, we are part of a global village where stewardship is not just an option but an inevitable and shared responsibility. Our series lays out the paths to a more balanced future, urging readers to act in concert to protect and nurture our world.

Each reader, whether they come from a scientific, policymaking, entrepreneurial, or simply a concerned perspective, is an integral part of the sustainability narrative. As we navigate the perils and potentialities of the Anthropocene, our capacity as humans to adapt, innovate, and ethically progress becomes more critical than ever.

The chapters within will guide you through a detailed exploration of our shared ecosystem and an investigation of the mechanics of change, intricacies of climate realities, promise of renewable energy, and imperative of water conservation, among other critical topics. Together, these themes constitute a mosaic of interconnected challenges and solutions, framing a world in which humanity's environmental legacy will be decided.

The overarching goal of this book—like the series itself—is to activate a collective awakening to the stakes that rest in the palm of our hands. It endeavors to marshal the collective ingenuity of our species in service of a resilient world where ecological empathy and innovation reign.

May the ideas enclosed here resonate with you and galvanize a new understanding of your role in the continuity of all life. We invite you to embrace this journey, as we reflect on the world we have shaped and envision the world we can co-create—a world where the health of our planet is inextricable from the prosperity of all its inhabitants.

As you turn these pages, I hope you will find not only a conduit for knowledge, but also a spark for lasting change. It is in the synthesis of ideas and the courageous application of them that our changing world will find its way to a harmonious symphony—one that is as resilient as it is beautiful.

With each step forward on this shared path, let us affirm our collective potential to be stewards of a balanced and thriving Earth—a legacy we must not only aspire to but actively build upon. Welcome to a journey of enlightenment, empowerment, and, ultimately, transformation.

Introduction and a Note from the Author

In the Preface, I extend an invitation—a fervent call to readers to distinguish yourselves not just as passive onlookers but as vital participants in steering the course of our collective future. This segment marks the fusion of personal insights with a broader narrative, a bridge between the dialogues initiated in the first installment of the *Our Changing World* series and the burgeoning discourse presented in this volume.

The motivation for this book is deeply rooted in a yearning to comprehend and articulate the complexities associated with the path toward sustainability. The journey began as a quest for knowledge, a deep dive into the heart of what it means to live sustainably on our dynamic planet, and quickly transformed into a peregrination of revelation and responsibility. It's an expedition that seeks to unravel the tapestry of ecological, economic, and social threads that, together, shape the fabric of our existence.

As the first book laid the foundation, it illuminated the imperative for change, setting the stage for this consequential narrative. The connection to that initial exploration emerges as a seamless continuum in which questions left unanswered now find their resolution, and the discourse is enriched with newly found depth and dimensions. It is a tale of growth—from awakening to action, from concept to creation.

Unlike other sustainability books that often dwell solely on doom and environmental nihilism, I bestow a lens focused on pragmatic optimism and innovation. This tome eschews the myopic view and instead adopts a holistic approach. It acknowledges the intertwining of ecosystems with economies and recognizes the cultural and personal attitudes that drive—and can potentially change—the course of our environmental impacts.

Herein lies a distinct departure point; this book does not merely echo a litany of challenges we face but rather elucidates the inspiring mosaic of solutions and the vanguards of change that are already molding a new epoch. Distilled within these pages is the subdued resonation of hope. It's a hope anchored not in wishful thinking but in actionable strategies ushered by the hands of humanity's collective ingenuity.

Emphasizing interconnectedness, the subsequent chapters unravel the many facets of sustainability, ranging from the incentives that drive renewable energy to the ethics surrounding the preservation of biodiversity. The narrative inherently fortifies the connection to the first book by transcending the introduction of these concepts and advancing a conversation through which we not only understand, but also apply interdisciplinary knowledge to our present conundrums.

The book differentiates itself through layers of narrative that do not merely explain, but also engage—bring you, the reader, into a participatory role. It spotlights how every individual holds power in myriad forms, be it as a policy influencer, a community leader, an entrepreneur, or even an informed consumer making sustainable choices. The stories contained herein are not abstract academic musings; they are the collective experiences of us all, positioned at the helm of today's turning tides.

Amid these chapters, the series' thematic lineage becomes clear: an unwavering belief in the potential of human creativity to adapt and innovate. This volume envisions a future where the intersection of technology and tradition coalesces to engender a sustainable symphony. In aligning our endeavors with nature and discarding the disjointed and fractured methodologies of the past, we cascade toward a harmony embedded within the rhythms of the Earth.

My intentions transcend the mere transfer of knowledge to an invocation for reflection, inspiration, and, ultimately, participation. This volume addresses the burgeoning landscape of sustainability with the hope readers will find not only a compendium of wisdom, but also a catalyst for personal and collective evolution.

In conceiving this oeuvre, my reflection roamed through the confluence of my experiences and the expansive literature in this field. From the realm of studies chronicling social movements to the nuances of technology's evolution, I've stitched a composition that distills quintessential truths and forward-thinking concepts into a digestible, engaging, and impactful narrative.

This book aims to cast a spectrum of light onto the oft-overlooked crannies where sustainability dwells. It's an ode to Earth's multitudes, an acknowledgment of the responsibility we share, and an unmistakable reminder of the boundless opportunities that await our collective embrace.

Lastly, this volume is a testament to the resolute spirit of those on the frontlines of this grand venture. To the environmental scientist deciphering climatic trends, the student sowing the seeds of advocacy, the policymaker navigating uncharted ethical landscapes, the renewable energy specialist innovating for a cleaner tomorrow, and to every single soul whose heartbeat resonates with a desire to safeguard our world—it's to you this book speaks.

Individually, we cast ripples upon the waters of change. Together, we can summon a tide powerful enough to reshape our world. I welcome you to join me in this endeavor—the pursuit of a more informed, vibrant, and sustainable existence—where each step we take becomes the legacy we leave.

Embracing Curiosity: A Conversation with Skeptics

In the journey toward understanding and implementing sustainable practices, skepticism is inevitable. This section isn't about confronting skepticism but rather engaging with it. It's about embracing the inherent curiosity that drives skeptics to question what they're told about environmental issues, the green economy, and sustainability in general. Skeptical interrogation, after all, can be a forceful ally in refining our ideas and strategies to foster a more resilient world.

Environmental skepticism can manifest in many forms—from those who doubt the severity of environmental problems to those who question the efficacy of proposed solutions. Often, skeptics demand evidence, rigor in research, and compelling arguments to be convinced of the need for change. This can inspire thorough investigation and innovation within the scientific community and technology sectors engaged in environmental studies and applications. Engaging with skepticism provides a platform to confront the very myths that hamper progress and erode trust in scientific consensus.

To forge a productive dialogue with skeptics, we must first understand their perspective. Is their skepticism rooted in a lack of information, conflicting information, or perhaps a deep-seated ideology? Rather than dismissing their concerns outright or bombarding them with data, it's vital to listen, show empathy, and attempt to understand what drives their skepticism. Science matters, but so do the concerns of individuals and communities, and these need to be contextualized within a broader social discourse.

Conversations with skeptics must remain open and involve effective communication strategies. We need to frame our arguments in ways that resonate with the values of our audience, whether they are policymakers who prioritize economic growth or communities concerned about their ancestral lands. It's not just about proving a point; it's about creating an inclusive narrative that acknowledges the diverse interests and values of all stakeholders.

Engaging with skeptics is not a battle to be won but an opportunity to broaden the support base for sustainability initiatives. It's by recognizing the strength of diverse opinions and fostering a culture of continuous learning and improvement we can truly move forward. While not all skepticism can be quelled, each conversation held in good faith is a step closer to creating a collaborative environment essential for the kind of wide-scale change we aspire to achieve.

As we move forward in this book, exploring the nuances of our changing world and the imperatives of sustainability, let us remember dialogue with skeptics is integral to our collective progress. It provides a critical mirror to our assertions and helps us approach the grand challenge of sustainability with humility, rigor, and determination.

Series Overview: Exploring *Our Changing World* and its Central Ideas

After the foundational journey initiated in *Threads of Green: Weaving Sustainability into the Cultural Fabric*, where the intricate dance of cultural diversity and unity was explored as a cornerstone for achieving sustainability, our series, *Our Changing World*, advances into its next phase with *A Sustainable Civilization: Unraveling the Threads of Change*. Building upon the understanding that a sustainable future is unattainable without a deep appreciation for the myriad cultural perspectives influencing our environmental interactions, this second volume pivots toward the broader mechanisms of societal transformation. It aims to deepen our comprehension of how diverse cultures contribute essential wisdom and practices toward addressing the multifaceted challenges of our time—industrialization, population expansion, and rapid technological advancements—thereby marking a pivotal shift in our collective narrative toward embracing ecological interconnectedness.

As we proceed, *A Sustainable Civilization* enriches our series' discourse by weaving a more complex, yet coherent vision of sustainability that integrates ancient wisdom with contemporary innovation. This volume acts as a bridge, connecting the cultural insights and sustainable practices outlined in *Threads of Green* with the forthcoming exploration of ethics, multicultural perspectives, and the role of businesses in shaping a sustainable future. Here, the journey of *Our Changing World* series evolves, not just by layering additional dimensions of our relationship with the planet but by reinforcing the series' core premise: the path to a sustainable and just world is a collective endeavor that necessitates a fusion of knowledge, cultural respect, and systemic innovation. From here, the series will take the following exploration:

Threads of Green: Weaving Sustainability into the Cultural Fabric

Threads of Green presents a detailed examination of how cultural diversity and unity are essential to achieving sustainability. This book positions itself at the intersection of cultural studies and environmental science, arguing that a truly sustainable future cannot be realized without a deep understanding of the varied cultural perspectives that shape our interactions with the environment.

By tracing the evolution of cultural landscapes over time, the book showcases how traditions, beliefs, and practices from around the world offer unique insights and solutions to contemporary ecological challenges. It stresses the importance of integrating traditional wisdom with modern technological and scientific advancements to address these issues effectively. This fusion not only enriches our approach to sustainability but also ensures that solutions are culturally sensitive and widely applicable.

The narrative underscores the critical role of cultural diversity in enriching the global sustainability discourse. It illustrates how embracing the interconnectedness of global and local efforts is vital for the stewardship of our planet. Through stories of resilience, innovation, and collective action, *Threads of Green* highlights how cultural insights and practices contribute to building a sustainable world.

In essence, the book serves as a call to action for individuals, communities, and policymakers to recognize and harness the power of cultural diversity and integrated system thinking in crafting a sustainable future. It's an essential guide for anyone looking to understand the complex relationship between culture and sustainability, offering a rich perspective on how to weave these threads into the fabric of our everyday lives.

A Planet in Balance: Exploring the Socio-Cultural Landscape of Sustainability

A Planet in Balance provides a thorough examination of the intricate relationships between sustainability, ethics, and multicultural perspectives. The book investigates the ethical bases that support the pillars of environmental, social, and economic sustainability, presenting a nuanced discussion on how these ethical considerations are essential for understanding and advancing sustainability goals. It explores how individual values, cultural backgrounds, and societal frameworks critically shape our perceptions and engagements with sustainability.

Central to the book's discourse is the vital role that education, art, and storytelling play in enhancing sustainability awareness and motivating societal action. These elements are portrayed as powerful tools for bridging the gap between knowledge and action, effectively engaging diverse audiences and fostering a deeper connection to sustainability issues.

The narrative further extends into the realm of global governance and international cooperation, scrutinizing the mechanisms of policy development and the execution of international environmental agreements. This examination reveals the complexities and challenges of global collaboration, while also highlighting successful strategies that have led to meaningful progress in sustainability efforts.

By providing an in-depth analysis of how ethics, culture, and governance intersect with sustainability, *A Planet in Balance* offers a comprehensive perspective on the socio-cultural dimensions of sustainability. The book encourages readers to reflect on their roles within this global framework and inspires collective efforts toward achieving a sustainable and balanced planet.

The Responsibility Renaissance: Business as a Catalyst for Environmental and Social Ethics

The Responsibility Renaissance marks the culminating insight of the *Our Changing World* series, underlining how businesses are uniquely positioned to drive sustainability and ethical practices within the global marketplace. Advocating a significant paradigm shift, the book urges businesses toward adopting regenerative, waste-minimizing, and resource-efficient practices. It showcases the indispensable role of data and analytics in marrying business operations with environmental sustainability goals through insightful case studies and actionable insights.

Highlighting that sustainability efforts transcend mere ethical obligations to become strategic differentiators, the book offers a variety of strategies for businesses to embed eco-friendly practices across their operations. This encompasses leveraging cutting-edge technologies for sustainable supply chain management and innovating in product and service development.

Leadership's pivotal role in driving the sustainability agenda is underscored, emphasizing visionary leaders' capacity to integrate sustainability with innovation, ethical marketing, and impactful community engagement. The narrative stresses compliance with Environmental, Social, and Governance (ESG) standards as foundational to sustainable business development.

As an essential blueprint for businesses at any stage of their sustainability journey, *The Responsibility Renaissance* delivers a comprehensive framework for weaving environmental and social ethics into the fabric of business practices. Through theoretical exploration and practical examples, it charts a path for businesses striving to be at the forefront of corporate responsibility and sustainability, making it an indispensable resource for leaders and entrepreneurs alike.

The Backstory of the *Our Changing World* Series

What compels a person to delve into the deep river of sustainability, cultural geography, and executive leadership and to emerge with a story to tell? It is the richness of the world's cultural tapestry and the pressing urgency of our environmental crises that fuels the *Our Changing World* series, a narrative canvas I have woven with countless threads of knowledge and experience acquired over twenty years.

My voyage began over two decades ago on the familiar shores of academic rigor, within the bastions of public accounting and professional services firms. Here, the grasp of corporate sustainability strategy was not merely a trade; it was a craft honed through persistence akin to a blacksmith shaping iron. My tenure at prominent Big Four firms was merely the prologue to a much grander tale.

Academia and boardrooms could only teach me so much. It was outside, in the expanse of the living, breathing world, where I would uncover the most poignant lessons. I traversed the globe, journeying through Indigenous territories, sitting with elders, listening to stories of lived experiences from the people living in these remote villages, and understanding the vital pulse of sustainability beat strongest within the communities that have revered the Earth long before the term "sustainability" was even coined.

Amidst these encounters, the inkling that Western ideologies and Indigenous knowledge could converge grew into a bold conviction. As a cultural geographer, I sought to explore not just the physicality of places, but the ethereal sense of "place" embedded in the narratives and rituals that define human-environment interactions.

This exploration transformed me, carving into my consciousness the necessity of a holistic outlook. I saw not only the fragility of nature but the resilience of cultures. Witnessing firsthand the intricate symbioses between communities and their lands, I was heartened by the demonstrated potential for both conservation and sustainable development.

The more communities I visited, the more apparent it became that sustainability is as much about maintaining cultural identity as it is about promoting green technologies. This symphony of sustainability resonates on multiple frequencies—environmental, social, cultural, and spiritual. Each note is crucial for the harmony of the whole.

As I journeyed on, camera in hand and heart open, the diversity of our world unraveled before me in exquisite complexity. Through the lens, each photograph captured a story, a piece of wisdom, a moment where the dance of culture and nature was in perfect step.

My storytelling, thus, is not a mere recapitulation of facts and figures but an endeavor to touch the soul of the reader. The aromas, colors, and textures of distant lands must leap off the pages and draw one into a gentle embrace with the world's myriad societies and ecosystems.

The *Our Changing World* series is inspired by this wealth of discovery. It is a guided expedition that introduces renowned leaders, humble farmers, wise elders, and enterprising youths, all of whom share a common thread—they are the vanguards of sustainability, each in their own right.

In the crafting of this narrative, my objective has never been to merely educate. It has been to awaken a sense of wonderment and responsibility, to ignite the flame of activism within each reader, and to rally a community of kindred spirits that will champion the cause for a sustainable planet.

This is a tale of unity in which science and story coalesce. The scientific underpinnings are undeniably crucial—they provide the framework upon which our understanding of sustainability rests. But the story is the heart, beating life into the framework and inspiring action.

The *Our Changing World* series, therefore, is not a single chorus but a tapestry of voices—a multidisciplinary narrative that seeks to connect the pragmatic solutions of scientific inquiry with the emotional impetus that only a compelling story can provide.

My aim is to capture and translate the soul of sustainability as I have experienced it: in the boardroom and in the wild, in policy and in practice. It is to lay bare the intrinsic connections that interweave humanity with the broader ecology of the Earth.

Thus, each chapter in this series serves as a waypoint on a quest, beckoning readers to journey through the nexus of environment, culture, and leadership. It is an invitation to envision a new paradigm in which humanity thrives not apart from, but as a part of the natural world.

It's a narrative that asserts we are at our best when we recognize the interconnectedness of our world, champion diversity, and walk hand in hand toward sustainability. The *Our Changing World* series is my ode to our planet—a call to all who will listen to join in the dance of change and become stewards of a world that endlessly gives and asks only that we respect its delicate balance.

Chapter 1:
The Imperative for Change: Embarking on Sustainability

As we steady our gaze on a horizon fraught with environmental uncertainties, the call for a decisive pivot toward sustainability becomes compelling and essential. Grappling with the quagmire of degradation that shadows our planet's health and human prosperity, it's clear we're at a critical juncture—our actions (or inaction) today will echo through generations.

Pursuing a sustainable future demands a collaborative and scientifically informed approach that sweeps across the complex tapestry of ecological, economic, and societal domains. By harnessing innovative solutions and embracing transformative changes, we begin a journey emboldened by the resilience of our natural world and the indomitable human spirit.

Embedded within each step toward this shared vision lies the acknowledgment of the delicate balance we must maintain and the collective responsibility that every stakeholder bears. It's not an understatement to assert that embarking on sustainability isn't merely an option—it's an imperative, an urgent call to action that resonates with the depth of our understanding and the breadth of our capacity to effect change.

The Sustainability Imperative: Why It Matters

In weighing the fate of our world, the need for a sustainable future is not just advisable; it's vital. The "Sustainability Imperative" is the conviction driving us toward respecting our planet's finite resources while aiming for equity and economic vitality. This imperative underpins the rationale for a seismic shift in how we live, produce, and consume. It's not an option; it's a prerequisite for the long-term survival of civilization and ecosystems alike.

At its core, sustainability focuses on meeting the needs of the present without compromising the ability of future generations to meet their own needs. This goal is no trite aspiration but an urgent clarion call—a warning that plays out daily as climate change intensifies, resources dwindle, and biodiversity contracts.

The science is unequivocal: the Earth's systems are strained, verging on thresholds beyond which recovery may not be possible. Climate change, an existential threat, affects everything from global weather patterns to the health of the poorest communities who are most vulnerable to such changes. Thus, pursuing sustainability is not only environmentally and ethically appropriate, but also forms a bulwark against human hardship.

Transitioning to sustainable practices carries economic imperatives as well. As traditional resources become scarcer and costlier, economies must adapt to new, sustainable technologies and sources of raw materials. The change represents not just conservation of the environment but an evolution in economic development—a potential source of jobs, innovation, and resilience against the shocks of resource scarcity.

Furthermore, the call for sustainability transcends environmental conservation—it is a call for social justice. Often, the communities that contribute the least to global environmental problems are the ones that suffer the most. Sustainable development implies creating systems that allow for equitable access to resources, opportunities for all, and a fair distribution of the economic benefits of prosperity. It's about fostering a sense of global citizenship in which everyone has a stake in the health of our planet.

Moreover, the cultural dimension of sustainability cannot be overlooked. Our diverse cultures are deeply interlinked with the natural world—many derive identity, practices, and beliefs from the environment. As such, protecting ecosystems and fostering biodiversity also protects cultural diversity, ensuring a rich tapestry of human expression and knowledge for future generations.

Certainly, we can't tackle what we don't understand. Education and information are critical to galvanizing action and enabling people to make informed choices. A public that understands the interconnections between their actions and the environment and that recognizes the urgency to change forms the backbone of a movement toward sustainability. It's about engendering a culture that values sustainability as a core principle of citizenship.

In essence, sustainability is an integral aspect of human rights; it reflects our respect for each other and the generations that will follow. It's imperative that we work toward sustainable solutions that protect our planet, ensuring all life can thrive today and in the millennia to come. This Sustainability Imperative is, therefore, the very script upon which our future must be written.

Advocates and leaders in the myriad fields relevant to this existential task must now come forward to cast a vision that marries feasibility with ambition and speaks to both the heart and the analytical mind. For if we falter in our endeavor for a sustainable globe, we falter not just as individual nations or species but as a collective living on the lone spaceship we call Earth.

At this juncture, we can no longer view the Sustainability Imperative as a mere chapter in our history; it is the encompassing narrative of our time. It demands of us to act with an unwavering commitment, guided by the profound recognition that the Earth's bounty is not inexhaustible and its tolerance not unending. It's a commitment that must be lived out not just in words but in the very fabric of how societies operate and individuals live their day-to-day lives.

A Holistic View: Sustainability Across Domains

Within the terrain of sustainability lies a tapestry woven with the threads of multiple domains—economic, environmental, and social—all interconnected in the fabric of life. A holistic view does not merely observe these threads in isolation but understands the strength they provide when interlaced. Sustainability must, therefore, be approached from a comprehensive perspective, considering the influence and interplay across these domains in order to facilitate systemic change.

The economic domain is often seen as a rival to environmental conservation, yet in truth, the economy flourishes when it aligns with sustainable practices. Clean technologies and green industries open new markets and job opportunities, driving economic growth while safeguarding our planet. Businesses that innovate to reduce their environmental impact are often rewarded with reduced costs, enhanced reputation, and a loyal customer base that values sustainability. Conversely, ignoring sustainability can lead to financial risks from depleting resources or regulatory penalties.

From an environmental standpoint, a holistic approach to sustainability embraces the intrinsic value of ecosystems, going beyond the commodification of nature. It involves protecting biodiversity, preserving natural habitats, and understanding our dependence on the environment for services such as clean air and water, pollination, and climate regulation. This domain also tackles the urgent crises of climate change, ocean health, and land degradation, compelling us to act for the long-term viability of our natural world.

The social domain underscores the centrality of community well-being and equity in the sustainability equation. It recognizes a society cannot be truly sustainable if social injustices persist. Improving community well-being includes eradicating poverty and hunger, ensuring education and gender equality, and providing fair opportunities for all. At the heart of this domain is the belief that sustainability should leave no one behind and cater to the needs of the present without compromising the potential of future generations to meet their own needs.

Seamlessly integrating these domains demands systemic thinking and moving away from siloed strategies to a collective and collaborative approach. One such integrative approach is the concept of the circular economy—an economic model designed to minimize waste and make the most of resources. Shifting from linear production models to a circular system can significantly reduce environmental impact while catalyzing economic growth and social development.

Education and awareness-raising are critical in forging a holistic path to sustainability. By incorporating sustainability principles across educational curriculums, we can nurture an informed citizenry equipped to drive change in all domains. Moreover, active engagement with diverse stakeholders—including governments, businesses, non-profits, and the public—is essential in developing policies and strategies that recognize the interconnectivity of economic, environmental, and social factors.

Technological innovation is another crucial element in a holistic sustainability paradigm as it can offer tools to tackle challenges across domains. From renewable energy systems to smart agricultural practices, technology holds the potential to revolutionize our approach to sustainability. However, such innovations must be guided by careful consideration of their societal impacts and ethical implications to ensure they contribute positively to all domains of sustainability.

The holistic approach also necessitates cultivating a sustainability-oriented culture in which individual and collective actions align with the overarching goals. Such cultural shifts can be accelerated by leading by example—thought leaders, changemakers, and institutions that adopt sustainable practices inspire others within their sphere of influence to follow suit. Moreover, recognizing personal lifestyle choices, such as diet, transportation, and consumption, have far-reaching implications across domains is vital for building a sustainability-centric community ethos.

Similarly, urban and rural development must be reframed through the lens of sustainability, wherein city planning and rural initiatives prioritize green spaces, biodiversity, renewable energy, and efficient resource use. Such planning can deliver substantial environmental benefits, bolster economic resilience, and improve social well-being.

In sum, a holistic view of sustainability requires us to transcend traditional boundaries and embrace interdisciplinary thinking. By considering the economic, environmental, and social domains concurrently, we can craft comprehensive, robust solutions that not only mitigate the pressing issues of today, but also lay the foundation for a resilient and thriving planet for future generations. This integrated perspective is the keystone of our collective journey toward a sustainable future.

Forward Vision: Paving a Sustainable Path

As we've established the urgent need for a concerted move toward sustainability, it becomes critical to pave a path that is not only clear but achievable. The journey requires fortitude, informed by science and inspired by a shared vision of the future. With eyes set firmly on the horizon, this section illuminates the road ahead, forecasting the potential of a world that embraces sustainability instead of being stifled by shortsightedness and inertia.

Envisioning a sustainable future isn't merely daydreaming; it involves detailed planning and the consideration of multifaceted variables that influence our society. Whether it's energy, economics, or equity, the balance is delicate and imperative. The forward vision is grounded upon the three pillars of sustainability: the environmental, the economic, and the social. Each plays a vital role in ensuring progress in one area doesn't come at the cost of another.

From an environmental standpoint, the transition toward renewable energy and the conservation of biodiversity are not just idealistic goals; they are prerequisites for the enduring health of our planet. Empirical evidence urges us to keep global temperature rise below crucial thresholds, necessitating immediate and sustained reductions in greenhouse gas emissions. It also calls for protecting the myriad forms of life that compose the Earth's rich tapestry. A sustainable path ensures economic growth harmonizes with planetary boundaries.

Economically, sustainable development can no longer be seen as a hindrance to growth but rather as a stimulant of innovation. A forward vision envisages economies that thrive on circular principles, championing reuse and efficiency over depletion and waste. It imagines a world where green jobs outnumber those reliant on fossil fuels and financial markets reward long-term value creation that accounts for environmental and social impact.

The social dimension of sustainability interlocks the environment with the economy, emphasizing the importance of human well-being. This includes equitable access to natural resources, fair trade, the eradication of poverty, and the inclusion of marginalized voices in decision-making processes. Education is the bedrock of this vision as it nurtures critical thinking and creates a populace that is not just environmentally literate, but also endowed with the skills to partake in a green economy.

Technological innovation plays a transformative role in enabling more efficient use of resources and reducing our ecological footprint. Sustainable technology isn't just about renewable energy sources; it also entails advancements in agricultural practices, water purification, waste management, and sustainable urban design. The forward vision recognizes technology as a catalyst for change, provided it is developed and deployed with due regard for potential risks and ethical considerations.

Moreover, policymaking is intrinsic to cultivating sustainable change. It requires the alignment of local, national, and global regulations and incentives that reward sustainable behavior and penalize unsustainable practices. Policies serving sustainability must be adaptable, evidence-based, and crafted in consultation with stakeholders from various sectors of society to ensure legitimacy and effectiveness.

Activating this vision also means redefining our understanding of success. Prosperity and quality of life cannot be expelled from the sustainability equation. How we measure progress needs a profound shift, moving away from GDP as the sole metric toward more holistic indices that reflect the well-being of people and the health of our ecosystems.

As we ride the crest of the Anthropocene epoch, embracing our ability to impact the Earth positively is critical. A sustained, collective effort, one that is replete with education, advocacy, and action, is necessary. The forward vision is inherently optimistic and fueled by relentless hope that society will coalesce around the common goal of a future that is safe, equitable, and verdant.

A sustainable path is not only desirable, but also the only viable strategy for long-term human survival and prosperity. It's a path littered with challenges as well as abundant opportunities. The intersection of science, ethics, and policy will be the battleground where the fate of our planet is contended, and it is here our resolve must be the staunchest.

Ultimately, paving a sustainable path is an investment in continuing our story on this Earth. When future generations look back, let them say we saw the imperative for change and we rose to meet it with a vision that was both courageous and full of conviction.

Chapter 2:
Lessons from History:
Tracing Our Sustainable Roots

The roots of sustainability are deep, stretching back to practices embedded in the fabric of ancient civilizations—long before the term "sustainability" entered our lexicon. In tracing these roots, we discover a rich mix of innovation and respect for the natural world that guided our ancestors' existence.

This chapter excavates these historical practices and examines how early societies from diverse geographies thrived by ingeniously managing resources, thereby ensuring their longevity. From ancient agriculture that worships the cycles of nature to Indigenous knowledge systems that prioritize harmony with the environment, this exploration illuminates how such time-tested approaches can inform our current sustainability crisis.

With keen awareness, we learn the principles guiding sustainable practices—cyclical resource use, diversity preservation, and dynamic equilibrium—are not new concepts but rather forgotten practices that need rekindling in our modern era. Unearthing these paradigms offers us a guidepost for imagining a future in which humanity once again lives in confluence with the Earth's systems, fostering resilience against the burgeoning pressures of the Anthropocene. Through a panoramic lens, this chapter highlights that while technology and innovation are indispensable, revisiting and integrating historical environmental stewardship is paramount for steering us toward a sustainable future.

The Industrial Leap: Consequences on Progress

The Industrial Revolution marked a time of transformative change that reshaped societies with the might of mechanized power and irrevocably altered humanity's relationship with the planet. As we stand on the brink of our modern era, it's imperative to grasp the ecological ramifications this leap into industrialization propelled in order to forge a sustainable future.

Industries burgeoned, fueled by coal and later oil, spinning factories that became the epicenter of human progress. Yet, this progress came with a hidden invoice—one the natural environment has been footing ever since. Air filled with soot, waterways poisoned with effluents, and a sky increasingly veiled by greenhouse gases depicts the grim portrait of industrialization's legacy.

The advancement of technology and industry during the Industrial Revolution gave rise to unprecedented economic growth. However, this growth was lopsided, largely benefitting a select few while laying burdensome costs on the environment—a currency of degradation and depletion that is still being tallied today.

Invisible rivers of emissions coursed through our atmosphere, leading us to the present predicament of climate change. The past gears of progress operated oblivious to their carbon footprints, unleashing knotted issues we unravel to this day. Our Earth's climate system, once a steady backdrop to human activity, has now become unpredictable and increasingly hostile.

Biodiversity, the intricate tapestry of life on Earth, faced unrivaled threats as habitats were fragmented and species lost to the great churn of industrial machinery. The splintering of ecosystems was more than an environmental concern; it was an omen of the intricate dependencies within the natural world that humans had chosen to ignore.

As industries claimed a stake in lands and resources, local communities faced relocation and were stripped of their traditional rights and sustainable practices. Indigenous knowledge, honed over centuries and deeply symbiotic with nature, was overshadowed by the juggernaut of modernization.

The lure of industrialization also ushered in mass urban migrations, giving rise to cities teeming with life yet strained by shortages and waste issues. Urban centers, the heart of industrialization's advance, paradoxically became both engines of opportunity and landscapes of exploitation and pollution.

With consumption's sharp spike, waste generation soared proportionately, birthing a legacy of pollution, the scale of which humanity had never before encountered. Thus began the cycle of use and discard, propelling our civilization toward a disposable culture widely at odds with sustainability principles.

The promise of infinite progress, a mantra of the industrial epoch, encountered the finite realities of planetary boundaries. As production scaled, renewable resources were overtaxed, and exponential exploitation led to scarcities where there were once abundances.

Yet, in the wake of industrialization, seeds of resistance and awareness were also sown. Workers pushed back against inhumane conditions, leading to the rise of labor rights. Simultaneously, the strain on natural resources gestated early environmental consciousness, giving birth to conservation movements.

The social constructs of the Industrial Age, centered around wealth production and material accumulation, cast a long shadow over societal values. This shift laid the groundwork for today's introspection into what constitutes true progress and well-being. Sustainable development requires us to redefine these very constructs, assigning an intrinsic value to nature rather than a mere instrumental one.

Mitigating the consequences of our industrial past demands reevaluation not only of practices but beliefs. It asks for an acknowledgment that humanity can't extract itself from the web of life and that the anthropocentric worldview that propelled the industrial era must evolve.

Reflecting upon this historical juncture reminds us our trajectory is not irreversible. The same ingenuity that birthed the industrial age holds the potential to catalyze sustainable solutions. It's an invitation to balance human aspirations with ecological prudence—an alien concept during the revolution but a mission critical to our survival now.

As we look to emerge from the shadows of the industrial age, embracing the sustainable roots of our past can light the path ahead. The lessons learned are our guiding stars: Progress need not be the adversary of preservation, and in the delicate dance between consumption and conservation, there is yet room for a harmonious step forward.

In concluding this exploration of the Industrial Revolution's impact, we observe that the imprint left on our Earth is as profound as it is endurant. Recognizing these scars offers us the clarity and resolve to heal, mend, and reimagine our approach to progress. Our future depends not on rejecting industrialism's fruits but on cultivating them harmoniously with the Earth's rhythms.

The Dawn of Conservation: Transitioning Toward Ecology

As the smog-filled skies of the Industrial Revolution slowly gave way to the serene vistas of the early twentieth century, a fresh understanding began to sprout within the human consciousness. This was a time of profound transformation in which the rise of conservation efforts marked an evolutionary step in how we interact with our natural environment. However, this wasn't a mere shift in attitudes; it represented an intellectual and practical transition toward the concepts and tenets of ecology.

The efforts of pioneering naturalists and foresters like Gifford Pinchot and John Muir underscored the imperative need for sustainable management of natural resources. These early conservationists laid the groundwork for a more complex, comprehensive approach to understanding the interdependence of life and the need to preserve biodiversity. Aldo Leopold's land ethic and Arthur Tansley's ecosystem concept scientifically illuminated these ideas. They sowed the seeds from which modern ecological consciousness would grow, a shift beyond mere resource conservation to embracing the intricate web of ecological relationships. This legacy serves as an invitation for us to continue exploring new dimensions of sustainability within the complex systems of our living world and inspire actions to address pressing environmental issues while maintaining the integrity of the countless species with whom we share our Earthly home.

Origins and Development of Conservation Thinking

Within the long the course of human history, the concept of conservation is a relatively recent thread, emerging from the convergence of foresight, necessity, and altruism. At its inception, conservation thinking was an answer to the unrestrained exploitation of natural resources spurred by industrialization. Pioneers of this philosophy recognized the bleak future that awaited the world if humanity continued on a path of environmental neglect. This section delves into the profound origins and gradual evolution of conservation as a transformative paradigm in human-environment interactions.

The cradle of conservation can be traced back to several ancient civilizations that practiced rudimentary resource management forms. However, it wasn't until the mid-nineteenth century that conservation coalesced into a coherent social and political ideology. To connect with this lineage, we must first turn our eyes to visionaries such as George Perkins Marsh, whose seminal work, *Man and Nature*, published in 1864, became a clarion call for the importance of preserving the Earth's resources for future generations.

Marsh's work, rich in forethought and dire warnings, was pivotal. It laid the groundwork for others, such as John Muir who would expand on these ideas with a distinct blend of spirituality and environmentalism. Muir's advocacy for protecting America's wilderness culminated in the foundation of the Sierra Club in 1892, an organization dedicated to preserving the country's natural wonders.

This budding conservation ethos was matched by pragmatic concerns during the Progressive Era in the United States, which spanned from the 1890s to the 1920s. Recognizing the rapid depletion of forests and wildlife, Former President Theodore Roosevelt and his chief forester, Gifford Pinchot, ignited a new phase of conservation action. Their policies sought not just to preserve wilderness but to establish a sustainable yield approach to resource use, a concept that had profound implications for national forest management and public land policies.

In the early twentieth century, conservation thinking spread, taking root in multifarious ways across different societies. In Europe, scientific forestry had already introduced conservation principles, emphasizing balance and regeneration. Simultaneously, in African and Asian colonies, the imposition of Western conservation models often clashed with Indigenous ways of life, highlighting the complex relationship between conservation and cultural dynamics.

The interwar years saw conservation thinking continue to develop, albeit less prominently. Economic strains and global tensions pushed environmental concerns to the periphery of the international agenda. However, during this period, the theoretical underpinnings of conservation expanded and deepened, setting the stage for a resurgent movement after World War II.

As the world emerged from the conflict and the ensuing reconstruction gave way to unprecedented economic growth, the limits to this progress started to show. Rachel Carson's landmark book, *Silent Spring*, published in 1962, voiced growing anxieties about pollution and the wanton use of pesticides. Her work reverberated around the globe, awakening a consciousness regarding human vulnerability to environmental harm and the interconnectedness of life.

Carson's efforts fostered a stronger and more scientifically informed conservation ethic. They also played a pivotal role in the burgeoning environmental movement of the 1960s and 1970s, which began to elevate conservation from a primarily utilitarian and scientifically grounded effort to a moral and ethical imperative.

Conservation diverged from its roots in natural resource management, embracing broader ecological concepts. The 1970s witnessed profound shifts, with the formation of organizations such as Greenpeace and the establishment of pivotal moments like the first Earth Day. Conservation thinking was now enmeshed with a new ecological awareness characterized by a holistic view of Earth as a single, interdependent system.

The evolution of conservation reached the international stage with the Stockholm Conference in 1972, the first United Nations conference on the human environment. This event marked an acknowledgment of environmental issues as globally significant and crucial for peace, security, and development.

This era also witnessed the rise of landmark environmental legislation, such as the Endangered Species Act of 1973 in the United States, which symbolized a shift from utilitarian conservation aimed at managing resources for human use to a new ethos that also recognized intrinsic value in other forms of life. It acknowledged a sense of stewardship over nature, a belief that humanity is responsible for the well-being of the planet's biodiversity.

As we approached the turn of the millennium, sustainable development emerged as a shared goal articulated in the Brundtland Commission's report *Our Common Future* in 1987. The report's definition of sustainable development as meeting "the needs of the present without compromising the ability of future generations to meet their own needs" married the concepts of conservation and development.

Now, in the twenty-first century, conservation thinking has branched out, addressing complex challenges like climate change, habitat destruction, and loss of biodiversity. These issues demand multifaceted approaches that integrate scientific understanding, cultural wisdom, economic viability, and global cooperation.

This journey through conservation's past highlights our adaptive and responsive capabilities as a species, showcasing our potential to harmonize our existence with the natural world. As we grapple with the intricate challenges of our age, the lessons gleaned from the development of conservation thinking serve as a beacon of hope and a guiding framework for our continued efforts to preserve the planet. This quest, born from a convergence of awareness, empathy, and necessity, encapsulates humanity's enduring endeavor to live sustainably on the Earth that nurtures us all.

The Shift from Conservation to Ecology: Why it Happened

As we delve deeper into the intricacies of our relationship with the natural world, it becomes essential to understand the pivotal shift from a conservation-centric view to one deeply rooted in ecological principles. The reasons behind this transition are multifaceted, embedding themselves within the realms of increased scientific understanding, socio-political changes, and a burgeoning awareness of our planet's limitations and interconnections.

Conservation was traditionally concerned with the protection of particular species or habitats, borne from an era in which the majesty of nature was often seen primarily as a resource to be used wisely for human benefit. These efforts were laudable and necessary, laying the groundwork for the preservation of countless species and landscapes. However, as time marched on, we realized the conservation model, with its focus on the singular preservation of parts, was not sufficient to address the complex interplays that shape life on Earth.

This awakening was, in part, a scientific revolution—a paradigm shift stimulated by ecosystem ecology's emergence. Ecosystem ecology presented the tenet that life is not a collection of discrete entities but rather a tapestry of inextricably linked systems and processes. It showcased the inherent value of relationships between organisms and their environments, thus, altering the course of environmental thought.

Economic development and global industrialization had been altering landscapes at an unprecedented rate, prompting scientists to signal the unintended consequences of these transformations. The realization that human actions were causing widespread shifts in ecological balances lent urgency to the need for a holistic approach, one that transcended the boundaries of traditional conservation.

Simultaneously, major socio-political events, such as the publication of Rachel Carson's *Silent Spring* in 1962, galvanized public consciousness. It instilled a palpable fear and concern for the impacts of unchecked industrial activities on natural systems and human health. This, among other influential works, elevated the discussion from the level of practical resource management to that of ethical consideration for all forms of life.

Further impetus for the shift toward ecology came from a growing body of evidence that demonstrated the interconnectedness of natural systems. As researchers began to understand phenomena such as biodiversity loss, climate change, and the decline of ecosystem services, conservationists increasingly recognized that protecting individual species or habitats was not enough. Ecosystem-based management became essential for maintaining the integrity of nature's synergy.

The development of ecological theory also brought forward key concepts such as carrying capacity, limitations to growth, and sustainability. These ideas emphasized that, rather than focusing merely on conservation, strategies must facilitate the coexistence of human and natural systems in a way that is maintainable over the long term.

Legislation and policy, too, felt the reverberations of this ecological enlightenment. From the establishment of the Endangered Species Act to international agreements like the Convention on Biological Diversity, there was a progressive recognition that laws and guidelines must reflect the complexity of ecosystems if biodiversity is to be truly preserved.

An ethical dimension also colored the shift toward ecology. A broader ethical stance that sought to recognize intrinsic value in all of nature, not just the parts of it deemed useful to humans, began to influence conservation ideologies. This biocentric approach laid the groundwork for an ecological ethic, a moral framework that tears down the barrier of human exceptionalism and advocates for a deep respect for all life forms.

The communication of ecological science played no minor role in this transition. As environmental education and media coverage grew, so too did the general public's ecological literacy. Knowledge was no longer locked within academic realms; it became a shared asset that shaped the discourse on environmental protection and sustainability.

This increasing appreciation for the myriad ecosystem services—such as water purification, climate regulation, and pollination—meant their preservation became an issue of self-interest for human societies. The intricate balance of natural systems was no longer an abstract concept; it became a cornerstone of a sustainable future.

Finally, the holistic view of ecology brought with it a commitment to an interdisciplinary approach. Recognizing that environmental issues were entangled in the complex web of politics, economics, culture, and technology, solutions required collaboration across various sectors and disciplines. The field of ecology became the meeting ground for such diverse expertise, underscored by a shared mission to understand and preserve the inherent balance of the natural world.

As the conservationist mindset evolved into a more ecologically focused narrative, it brought about a fundamental change in how we perceive and interact with nature. Capturing the essence of this shift is key to forging a path toward sustainable living, as it allows us to see beyond conservation's historical confines and appreciate the sophisticated dynamics of Earth's living systems.

The journey from conservation to ecology is a testament to the adaptability and growth of environmental thought. It's a response to the clarions of our changing world—a recognition that conserving pieces is not enough when sustainability demands we understand and preserve the whole. In this new paradigm, ecology offers a blueprint for a future in which human progress and natural harmony can exist in concert and sustainability is not just aspirational but foundational to our coexistence with the planet.

Understanding the Discipline of Ecology

Understanding the discipline of ecology is crucial in our journey toward sustainability. Its essence lies in the study of organisms, their environments, and the intricate web of interactions that bind them. At its core, ecology seeks to unravel the complex relationships between living beings and their habitats, explaining how these interactions shape the dynamics of natural systems. It's not just about identifying species and their behaviors; it's a deep dive into understanding how life thrives and adapts amidst the ever-changing tapestry of our planet.

Ecologists explore the patterns of life—from microscopic bacteria to sprawling ecosystems—and use this knowledge to appreciate how nature operates. They examine the way in which energy flows through environments and how matter cycles within ecosystems. Whether it's the decay of fallen leaves in a forest or the migration patterns of birds across continents, every process is a chapter in the narrative of our natural world that ecologists aim to read and comprehend.

Furthermore, the subject of ecology is pivotal in addressing environmental concerns. Through a deeper understanding of ecological principles, we can begin to grapple with issues such as habitat destruction, pollution, and climate change. It equips us with the insights to predict how these problems may affect the integrity of ecosystems and the services they provide to humanity and all other life forms on Earth.

Ecology isn't a discipline that exists in isolation; it is inherently interdisciplinary. It draws upon biology, geology, chemistry, meteorology, and many other fields to build a holistic view of how the natural world functions. It also informs our approaches in other related disciplines, like conservation biology and environmental science, framing the strategies we develop to preserve and restore natural environments.

The applications of ecological science are far-reaching. In agriculture, for example, ecological insights help farmers develop sustainable practices that work with—rather than against—natural processes. In urban planning, ecology guides the design of green spaces that offer respite to city-dwellers and habitats for urban wildlife, fostering a meaningful connection between people and nature.

One key component of ecology is the concept of ecosystems, which are communities of living organisms interacting with their physical environments. Each ecosystem—whether a vast ocean, a secluded pond, or a dense forest—is a product of numerous biotic (living) and abiotic (non-living) components working in tandem. As we delve into the study of these systems, we gain actionable knowledge on maintaining the delicate balance that sustains them.

Energy transfer and nutrient cycling are two essential themes within ecology. These processes demonstrate how ecosystems are powered and sustained. Ecologists track the flow of energy from the sun to producers and through the food web, while also monitoring how essential elements like carbon and nitrogen cycle through the environment. This knowledge is fundamental in appreciating how ecosystems function and what they require to remain healthy and productive.

The discipline also teaches us about population dynamics and community interactions. We learn how species populations grow, shrink, and fluctuate over time as they are influenced by factors like competition for resources, predation, and disease. It illuminates how communities of species exhibit symbiotic relationships—mutualism, commensalism, and parasitism—all adding to the complexity of ecological intrigue.

As we face a changing climate, the relevance of ecology intensifies. It aids in forecasting how species and habitats may respond to alterations in temperature, precipitation patterns, and extreme weather events. With this foresight, ecologists inform conservation efforts and climate adaptation strategies to bolster the resilience of ecosystems and the services they provide.

Additionally, ecology plays a vital role in informing policy. When environmental laws and regulations are crafted, the insights from ecological research can help balance economic needs with the preservation of ecological integrity. It offers a scientific foundation upon which sustainable resource management practices can be built, ensuring exploitation does not eclipse conservation.

Ecology contributes significantly to public health. By studying how diseases spread among populations and across species, we can develop better strategies for control and prevention. The understanding of ecosystems also assists in identifying the conditions that promote or hinder the transmission of diseases, leading to healthier environments for all.

This subject, although steeped in scientific rigor, transcends into the philosophic. It presents a profound reflection on our place within the natural order. It asks us to consider the ethics of our interactions with the rest of the living world and challenges us to foster a respectful and sustainable coexistence with nature.

To talk about ecology is to talk about connections. It serves as a reminder that we are but strands in the intricate web of life and that the health of our natural environment is intimately linked to our own well-being and survival. The discipline of ecology is not just about understanding nature; it's about understanding our home and how we can live in harmony with the myriad other forms of life with whom we share it.

In essence, the discipline of ecology anchors us in the reality of our interdependence with nature. It's a beacon guiding the way toward a sustainable future, one in which we recognize not only the inherent value of the natural world, but also our responsibility to protect it. By fostering an ecological consciousness, we can begin to build a legacy of stewardship for the Earth that honors the remarkable complexity and vitality of the systems that sustain us all.

Land Ethic: From Resource Use to Ecosystem Health

As we've journeyed through the evolution of ecological thinking, it's evident that a paradigm shift has occurred in how we interact with our terrestrial home. The utilitarian approach to land as a mere commodity serving human needs and economic interests has gradually given way to a more holistic appreciation of ecosystems and their intrinsic value. This transition is not just a theoretical ideal; it has become a critical prerequisite for sustainability and ecosystem resilience.

In the past, land was viewed primarily as soil—a static entity that could be endlessly exploited for agriculture, mining, and urban expansion. However, this perspective is fundamentally flawed. Ecosystems are dynamic and complex assemblies of plants, animals, and microorganisms interacting with their physical environment in delicate balances that foster life. The protective concept of land ethic places these systems at the center of conservation efforts, advocating a relationship of mutual respect between people and the land.

Implementing a land ethic means comprehending the ecological processes that maintain the health and productivity of landscapes. It involves acknowledging that human actions can disrupt these processes, leading to degradation and loss of biodiversity. Speaking to this, Aldo Leopold, the father of land ethics, famously wrote, "A thing is right when it tends to preserve the integrity, stability, and beauty of the biotic community. It is wrong when it tends otherwise." This mantra encapsulates the shift from viewing land as a resource bank to seeing it as a living, breathing organism deserving of ethical consideration.

The stewardship of land based on ethical principles requires a deep understanding of ecology. It demands comprehensive land use planning and management strategies that conserve soil, water, and biological resources. Characteristics of healthy ecosystems include rich biodiversity, self-renewal capacity, and resilience to disturbances like climate change. Unfortunately, this understanding wasn't always the cornerstone of our agricultural and industrial practices.

Today's era calls for the application of sustainability practices that reflect a modern land ethic. Sustainable land management (SLM) integrates land use planning, water management, biodiversity conservation, and the sustainable use of natural resources to meet human needs while ensuring the long-term viability of ecosystem services. For instance, agroforestry combines agriculture with tree cultivation to enhance soil health, increase biodiversity, and provide long-term income for rural communities. This is a practical example of the modern application of land ethic principles.

It's important to recognize that implementing a land ethic is not a sacrifice, but an investment in the future. Healthy ecosystems provide benefits far beyond the immediate ecological gains. They form the foundation of human well-being—securing food, clean water, and shelter—and offer cultural, spiritual, and recreational experiences that enrich our lives. This new interpretation of the land as a community to which we belong represents a milestone in achieving sustainable coexistence with the rest of the natural world.

This ethic plays a critical role in confronting climate change. A land ethic that embraces ecosystem restoration—such as reforestation, wetland rehabilitation, and soil conservation—also acts as a strategic carbon sequestration approach. Moreover, it contributes to climate resilience, ensuring ecosystems can buffer extreme weather events and provide safe havens for biodiversity as conditions change.

Incorporating land ethics into policy is as profound as it is necessary. Governments, communities, and individuals must be enlightened on the merits of sustainable land use policies that promote ecosystem health. This shift toward ecosystem-based management is evident in many international frameworks, such as the United Nations Sustainable

Development Goals, which call for urgent action to combat land degradation and foster biodiversity.

Essentially, as we adapt to modern challenges, the land ethic evolves as well. It's no longer an abstract ethos, it is now a guiding principle that is being integrated into laws, regulations, and management practices. We're learning to measure progress not just by the yield of the crop, but by the health of the ecosystem—a crucial change in how we value our planet. A sustainable future hinges on this very shift and the collective effort to embrace the land ethic in every sphere of human activity.

In conclusion, the shift from viewing land as a mere resource to a focus on ecosystem health is not just an academic or environmentalist ideal but a practical necessity in the age of the Anthropocene. Moving forward, embracing a land ethic will be central to our efforts to forge a sustainable path for humanity. It's a transformation that calls for the wisdom to conserve, the courage to restore, and the foresight to protect the very systems that sustain us.

The Green Uprising: Environmental Movement Milestones Across the World

The environmental movement has been a burgeoning force, cascading around the globe through a series of milestones that have collectively redefined humanity's relationship with nature. Commencing with the profound undertakings of Indigenous communities and their time-honored stewardship of the Earth, this journey through history reveals an evolving tapestry of activism and policy.

A pivotal outcry came from the publication of Rachel Carson's *Silent Spring* in 1962, igniting public consciousness of the harms of pesticides and industrial pollution. Later, the palpable spirit of the first Earth Day in 1970 marked a unified stand of 20 million people seeking environmental reform—a testament to the growing power of collective will. These episodes, among others, underscore significant strides in environmental advocacy, each echoing a resounding call to respect and preserve our natural world.

The Green Uprising isn't merely a reflection of the past; it's a clarion call that continues to inspire and mobilize movements today, ensuring sustainability remains at the forefront of our societal evolution.

Triggers and Key Events of the Environmental Movement

As our journey through the environmental movement's history unfolds, we must pause to deeply comprehend the catalysts and landmark occurrences that have bolstered this crusade. Environmentalism didn't ignite in a vacuum; rather, it was the result of numerous shocks to our collective consciousness from events that unveiled the brittle relationship between human activities and the planet's well-being. Instances such as the infamous 1969 Cuyahoga River fire, which became a symbol of rampant industrial pollution, and the Santa Barbara oil spill earlier that same year have captured public attention and galvanized support for environmental protections.

The publication of Rachel Carson's *Silent Spring* in 1962 can be pointed to as a definitive moment in environmental awareness. Carson's narrative relayed the perils of pesticide misuse and its alarming effects on wildlife, particularly the bald eagle, a national symbol. Her persuasive prose, laden with scientific acumen, stirred a rising swell of environmental concern among both the public and policymakers, sowing the seeds for the likes of the United States Environmental Protection Agency (EPA) and the ban on DDT in the years to come. More on Carson and *Silent Spring* momentarily.

In the wake of *Silent Spring*, the first Earth Day, spearheaded by Senator Gaylord Nelson on April 22, 1970, marked a watershed event, unifying an estimated 20 million Americans—students, activists, and ordinary citizens—in a powerful display of commitment to environmental stewardship. This collective awakening highlighted the urgency of environmental challenges and played a pivotal role in spurring significant legislation, such as the Clean Air Act, Clean Water Act, and the Endangered Species Act, all of which carved out a firm foundation for environmental governance in America.

Internationally, the movement solidified with events like the 1972 United Nations Conference on the Human Environment in Stockholm, acknowledged as the first major global forum to reconcile economic development with the need for environmental protection. Here was carved the notion that humankind bore a solemn duty to safeguard the Earth for future generations, an idea that would later permeate sustainability charters and protocols world over.

Throughout the late twentieth century, mounting scientific evidence of global warming and the depletion of the ozone layer served as further impetuses. The discovery of a gaping hole in the ozone above Antarctica in 1985 precipitated an unprecedented response, culminating in the landmark Montreal Protocol, an international treaty to phase out substances responsible for ozone depletion. This demonstrated that collaborative action on environmental issues was within reach.

Into the twenty-first century, the environmental movement has adapted to the complexities of climate change, shifting societal values, and technological innovation. Events like the 2015 Paris Agreement under the United Nations Framework Convention on Climate Change marked a new age of global commitment. It brought together 196 parties to set determined goals to mitigate the advancing specter of climate change and expedite the translation of promises into policy and practice.

The interplay of activism, science, and policy has undoubtedly been the engine that propels the ecological agenda forward. Grassroots movements have gained momentum, as seen with the rise of organizations like 350.org, Extinction Rebellion, and the youth-led Fridays for Future. These groups echo the zeitgeist, channeling society's increasing awareness into demonstrations, legal actions, and advocacy campaigns. They are testament to the fact that concern for the environment can traverse borders, languages, and cultural divides to unite humanity in a singular cause.

Yet, despite the triumphant narratives, the environmental movement must also contend with pushback from vested interests and political inertia. The tug-of-war between progress and regression elongates as each leap forward is met with resistance. This underscores the need for continuous vitality within the movement, ensuring the subtle balance tilts toward the sustainable stewardship of our world.

Understanding these triggers and key events is not a mere chronicle of the past; rather, it arms us with lessons for the future. Each occurrence serves as a beacon that guides the collective action required to preserve our planet. The story of the environmental movement is interwoven with resilience and hope. It is a narrative we must carry forward with indefatigable spirit and determination.

Significant Players and Their Contributions

In tracing the milestones of the environmental movement, it's crucial to recognize the contributions of significant players whose advocacy and innovations have served as the propellants of change. Think of each activist, scientist, policymaker, and innovator as a thread meticulously woven into the tapestry of environmental sustainability. These individuals have not only shifted public perception but have anchored the very essence of ecological urgency within our collective consciousness.

Another torchbearer for environmental advocacy has been Nobel laureate Wangari Maathai. Her establishment of the Green Belt Movement in the 1970s in Kenya not only combated deforestation, but also empowered women and promoted sustainable livelihoods through tree planting. Maathai's legacy is a clear example of how environmental action can also forge pathways to socioeconomic benefits.

While some have led through their written work and grassroots activism, others have contributed through the realms of science and technology. James Hansen, a climatologist and professor, testified before

Congress in 1988 about the effects of human activities on climate change in a pivotal moment that elevated the issue of global warming from scientific circles to the forefront of public policy debate.

Similarly, the role of entrepreneurs cannot be understated. Elon Musk's Tesla Company has dramatically influenced the auto industry by popularizing electric vehicles, encouraging a shift away from fossil fuels, and challenging existing automotive conventions. Musk's ventures in solar energy and battery storage also present transformative possibilities for scaling sustainable energy solutions.

The intersection of policy and environmental advocacy has also yielded influential contributors. Former Vice President Al Gore has been both a politician and a communicator of climate science, most notably through his documentary *An Inconvenient Truth* and his work with the Intergovernmental Panel on Climate Change, which together won the Nobel Peace Prize in 2007. Gore's efforts have been vital in popularizing understandings of climate change and urging collective action.

Environmental organizations, too, play a critical role in driving change. Groups like the Sierra Club, founded by naturalist John Muir in 1892, have been at the forefront of the environmental legislative battles, as well as promoting conservation and sustainable practices long before they were mainstream concerns.

It is likewise vital to acknowledge the role Indigenous communities played in the stewardship of natural environments. A rich body of research highlights not only their disproportionately high burden of environmental degradation, but also their profound wisdom and proven strategies in ecosystem management. The traditional ecological knowledge of Indigenous peoples has informed sustainable practices and increasingly gained recognition in global discussions on conservation and climate change.

Each of these figures and organizations demonstrates that the fabric of environmental sustainability is diverse and multifaceted. Personal advocacy, scientific contributions, policymaking, technological innovations, and community-based actions collectively contribute to the strength of the movement. As each entity leverages its unique capabilities toward the goal of sustainability, they serve as both inspirers and catalysts for broader societal transformation.

Still, as we chronicle these significant contributors, we must remain cognizant of the myriad unsung heroes: local activists, community organizers, educators, and everyday individuals whose daily practices and teachings imbue sustainability into the fabric of society. Their contributions, though perhaps not as widely recognized, are equally integral to the groundwork of the overarching environmental narrative.

In the end, the reverence for and valorization of such significant players and their contributions are not for the sake of mere accolade. Instead, their stories and successes are a call to arms—a beckoning for each of us to see ourselves as potential agents of change within this grand pursuit of a sustainable and resilient world.

Post-War Environmental Awakening: Silent Spring and Its Impact

The post-war era witnessed a burgeoning environmental consciousness that would fundamentally reshape public perception and policy toward the natural world. Among the influential moments in this epochal shift was the publication of Rachel Carson's *Silent Spring* in 1962, a seminal work that cannot be overstated in its importance. Carson's eloquent prose and rigorous scientific perspective brought to light the deleterious effects of pesticides—particularly DDT—on birds, wildlife, and humans.

Carson's narrative was more than simply a cautionary tale; it was a call to arms that invigorated an already simmering environmental movement. Her meticulous research unveiled the insidious chain of events that ensued from the indiscriminate use of pesticides, painting a future in which the eponymous silence would befall nature due to the absence of birdsong. It stirred a public outcry and fostered a surge of activism that influenced the course of environmental policy.

The impact of *Silent Spring* culminated in legislative action and a broader environmental governance. Under public pressure, the U.S. government initiated scientific inquiries into the concerns raised by Carson. This led to the establishment of the Environmental Protection Agency (EPA) in 1970 and the subsequent banning of DDT in the United States. Carson's work laid the intellectual foundation for the modern environmental regulatory landscape and furthered an understanding that human health is intimately connected to the vitality of ecosystems.

Carson's influence extended beyond the United States, stirring international discourse on pesticide use and regulation. This global conversation underscored the need for a nuanced approach to agricultural practices, one that considers long-term ecological balance alongside short-term pest control measures. *Silent Spring* became a linchpin in the emergence of integrated pest management as an environmentally sensitive approach to agriculture.

However, the implications of Carson's enunciations were not just confined to policy. They catalyzed an environmental education movement that emphasized the obligations humans have toward stewarding the Earth. This educational ripple effect expanded environmental curricula in schools and universities, fostering a generation of environmentally literate citizens and professionals that would champion sustainability in varied sectors.

Moreover, Carson's work facilitated a shift in how society perceived the relationship between economic development and environmental health. A newfound comprehension that these were not mutually exclusive objectives but interdependent facets of a holistic societal well-being began to take shape. This transition was critical in reframing environmental protection as an intrinsic component of economic planning and vice versa.

The legacy of *Silent Spring* reverberates in the current ethos that underscores sustainability—a tribute to the enduring influence of

Carson's vision. It imbued the sustainability discourse with a moral dimension, interlinking ethical considerations with scientific and policy initiatives. The book's impact is evident in contemporary sustainability movements and debates regarding human interventions in nature and our collective responsibility to future generations.

This awakening to environmental concerns also cultivated fertile grounds for new forms of activism. Grassroots organizations, as well as larger NGOs, drew inspiration from Carson's work to advocate for conservation, biodiversity, and environmental justice. They played a critical role in mobilizing citizen engagement and effectuating meaningful changes at the local, national, and global levels.

In sum, *Silent Spring* engendered a paradigmatic shift in our understanding of and interaction with the natural world. Its publication marked a turning point from ignorance and exploitation to awareness and care, significantly influencing environmental policies and practices. The ensuing transformation created the very foundations on which sustainable development is pursued today, highlighting our intrinsic connection and responsibility to the Earth's well-being.

Shaping Sustainability Ethics: The Modern Context

In decoding the mosaic of sustainability ethics within the modern context, we must recognize the foundation established by historical cognizance. The Green Uprising equipped society with the vocabulary of the environmental movement, making "sustainability" a household term, yet it's essential to note that with greater awareness comes the evolution of a dynamic ethical framework.

Today's context beckons a nuanced approach to sustainability that integrates the diverse and intangible aspects of human values, ecological mindfulness, and technological responsibility. This planet, vibrant and resilient, is not merely a reservoir of resources but a complex system in which life's interdependencies necessitate a moral compass oriented toward long-term stewardship and equitable resource allocation. Amidst rapid technological advancements and shifting societal paradigms, global citizens are called to exercise vigilant ethics, grounded in respect for natural systems and a commitment to rectifying past environmental injustices. As we continue to influence our planet's balances, we are poised to champion a narrative in which sustainability isn't just a reaction to the crisis, but an intrinsic element of human ethos, embedding environmental imperatives into every facet of decision-making. Wielding the lessons of our sustainable roots, we aim to sculpt an ethical framework conducive to a thriving Earth in which the symbiosis of human endeavors and natural ecosystems define our legacy.

Defining Environmental Ethics: Value and Respect for Nature

The burgeoning recognition of environmental ethics as a philosophical discipline is not only timely, but also imperative in an era when human activities exert unprecedented impacts on the planet. This critical framework amalgamates an understanding of the moral relationship between humans and the environment, urging us to reconsider how we value and respect nature.

Environmental ethics challenges the anthropocentric paradigm that regards humans as separate from and superior to the natural world. This outlook has long justified exploitative practices on the grounds of economic progress. However, as we come to terms with the widespread ecological decline, the question of intrinsic value surfaces: Does nature possess worth beyond its utility to human beings?

Many theories have been proposed to articulate the inherent value of nature. Biocentrism, for instance, assigns moral significance to all living things, advocating for their interests irrespective of their use to humans. Ecocentrism takes a broader view, arguing for the moral consideration of ecological wholes like species, ecosystems, and the biosphere.

The notion of respect for nature can be understood on multiple levels. There's an ethical imperative to maintain the integrity of natural processes and systems that support life. This extends to individual organisms and their habitats, as well as to the health of entire ecosystems and biotic communities.

Understanding the value of nature also compels us to acknowledge the interconnectivity of all life forms. Respect for nature involves not only preserving what currently exists, but also ensuring the viability of natural habitats and species for future generations. Here, the concept of sustainability emerges as a guiding principle, espousing a manner of living that maintains the conditions for ecological balance and diversity over the long term.

The role of environmental education is vital in instilling a sense of value and respect for nature. Through greater awareness and understanding, individuals can appreciate the interdependencies within ecosystems and the critical services they provide to humanity.

Legal and governmental frameworks are fundamental to safeguarding our natural heritage. Policies that embody environmental ethics are crucial in guiding human actions to mitigate harm and promote stewardship. This includes laws that protect endangered species, combat pollution, and manage natural resources sustainably.

Cultural narratives and practices also shape our ethical relationship with the environment. Many Indigenous cultures exhibit a deep reverence for nature, integrating its protection into their value systems and daily practices. These traditions provide valuable insights into ways of living that are deeply attuned to environmental well-being.

In recent decades, the rise of eco-philosophy has pushed the boundaries of environmental ethics further by questioning the fundamental premises of modern civilization. It critiques the underlying attitudes that have led to the current ecological crisis, proposing radical shifts in values and practices that create a more harmonious coexistence with nature.

Respecting nature also implies recognizing its limits and vulnerabilities. It's essential that we address not only the symptoms of environmental degradation, but also its root causes, which are often embedded in systems of production and consumption. This necessitates a profound reflection on our lifestyle choices and their ecological ramifications.

An ethic of care emerges as a powerful paradigm within environmental ethics. It promotes compassion, responsibility, and a commitment to protecting the Earth as one would care for a loved one. This perspective fosters a relational understanding in which humans are seen as participants within the web of life, rather than its overlords.

The burgeoning field of environmental ethics is, thus, not just an academic pursuit but a practical imperative. It calls upon all sectors of society—businesses, governments, communities, and individuals—to foster a more ethical relationship with the planet. The moral imperative to respect and value nature is foundational for achieving a sustainable future.

Embracing environmental ethics requires a shift in consciousness. This means moving away from short-term gains to long-term viability, from exploitation to nurture, and from indifference to deep ecological awareness. Indeed, it's about evolving our moral horizon to include the non-human world as an equal partner in our shared existence.

As we continue to grapple with the pressing environmental challenges of our time, the importance of defining, disseminating, and practicing environmental ethics becomes increasingly apparent. It's a journey of transformation that calls for collective wisdom, moral responsibility, and an unwavering commitment to the planet that sustains us all.

Key Philosophies and Theories in Environmental Ethics

The movement toward a harmonious relationship with our natural world rests upon a deep understanding of the ethical foundations that guide our interactions with the environment. Environmental ethics, a branch of philosophy that studies the moral relationship between humans and the environment, provides the moral compass for navigating the complexities of environmentally responsible living.

In the quest for sustainable futures, it is quintessential to contemplate our place in the natural world. The integral philosophy that underscores environmental ethics is the inherent value of nature. Unlike traditional ethical theories that center human well-being as the primary concern, environmental ethics argues for the moral consideration of non-human entities in their own right. This natural value is the basis for biospheric egalitarianism, which posits that all living beings have intrinsic value and deserve respect and moral consideration.

An outgrowth of this thinking is the land ethic, which Aldo Leopold famously represented by extending ethical considerations to land and ecosystems. The land ethic espouses a community-centric view. This idea regards humans as members of a broader biotic community, wherein each member—be it plant, animal, or geomorphic feature—plays an essential role in the health and stability of ecological systems.

Eco-centric or ecological ethics further the concept of environmental centrality by asserting that the ecosphere, rather than solely the biosphere, should be the basis of ethical concern. This viewpoint emphasizes the interdependence of all biological and abiotic elements of nature and suggests ecosystem health and integrity are vital considerations. Holism in environmental ethics parallels these thoughts, advocating for the ethical consideration of whole ecological systems and positing that the sum of the parts is crucially significant.

Another cornerstone of environmentally ethical thought is deep ecology, founded by Arne Naess in the 1970s. This philosophy calls for profoundly restructuring modern human societies, advocating a shift from anthropocentrism to deep ecological consciousness. Deep ecology encompasses bioegalitarianism and promotes the flourishment of all forms of life through ecological harmony.

Contrasting deep ecology is the anthropocentric or human-centered approach, which considers human interests as pivotal. The pragmatic theory of environmental ethics emerging from this viewpoint argues for conservation and sustainability based on human needs and benefit. However, such theories do not necessarily preclude environmental protection; instead, they see environmental stewardship's instrumental value in human survival and well-being.

Environmental virtue ethics, another crucial theory, equates ecological behavior with personal character attributes. This approach suggests sustainable environmental practices arise from cultivating virtues such as respect, humility, and responsibility toward the natural world. Individuals are then seen as stewards of nature, nurturing an ethic of care that promotes ecological harmony.

The discourse on environmental justice interlaces with environmental ethics, highlighting the intersection of social justice and environmental protection. This perspective scrutinizes and challenges the uneven burdens of environmental degradation that marginalized communities often bear. It demands equitable distribution of environmental risks and amenities, emphasizing the ethical implications of environmental policy and practice on human well-being.

Ecofeminism, which unites ecological advocacy and feminist theory, scrutinizes the patriarchal structures that have dominated both women and nature. This philosophy draws parallels between the exploitation of the natural world and the subordination of women and seeks liberation from oppressive power dynamics for both.

Within these theories lies the precautionary principle, a policy guide in environmental decision-making. It promotes caution in the face of uncertainty and aims to prevent harm to the environment and human health, even if there are no conclusive scientific proofs of damage. This principle is instrumental in navigating ethical dilemmas by placing the responsibility on proponents of potentially harmful activities to prove their safety.

Existential phenomenology, while not exclusively an environmental theory, contributes to environmental ethics by focusing on the lived experience of human interaction with nature. It prompts a reflective understanding that can foster a more intimate, reverent, and responsible engagement with the natural world.

Bridging the gap between theory and practice, environmental pragmatism eschews the absolutist positions that can stymie environmental policymaking. Instead, it suggests practical, pluralist solutions to environmental issues that accommodate a variety of ethical positions and practical exigencies.

Each of these philosophies contributes a vital perspective to environmental ethics. Whether converging on the intrinsic value of nature or focusing on the pragmatic benefits to humanity, these frameworks offer rich, conceptual soil from which policies, practices, and personal beliefs can grow. Guided by these principles, every choice and action takes on deeper significance to express our collective moral standing with the Earth.

Ethical Dilemmas in Environmental Decision Making

In pursuing a sustainable future, ethical considerations must hold a position of prominence in our deliberations and actions. The choices we make today have staggering implications for not only the present generation, but also countless generations to come. As environmental decision-making becomes increasingly complex, it is rife with dilemmas in which, often, the ethically correct path is convoluted and contentious.

Take, for instance, the challenge of balancing economic growth with ecological preservation. Emerging economies strive for development to lift their populations out of poverty, yet this development may come at the cost of environmental degradation. Here lies an ethical quandary: Do we prioritize immediate human needs or long-term environmental health? It is a negotiation between the urgencies of the present and the uncertainties of the future that raises profound moral questions about equity and justice.

Another ethical dilemma emerges when we consider the distribution of environmental burdens. Often, it is the marginalized communities that are disproportionately affected by industrial pollution, land degradation, and climate change, despite contributing the least to these global issues. This inequity raises the question of how to ethically distribute the costs and responsibilities of environmental protection. Hence, decision-makers are compelled to navigate the murky waters wherein moral responsibility intersects with socio-political dynamics.

In the realm of wildlife conservation, the decision to prioritize certain species for protection over others raises another suite of ethical questions. Endangered species policies must weigh the value of a species against the economic interests it may impede. Here, intrinsic values of biodiversity come face to face with the instrumental values of economic utility, each vying for supremacy in the decision-making calculus.

Technological advancements in renewable energy and geoengineering present their ethical dilemmas as well. While these innovations hold the potential to mitigate climate change, they are also fraught with risks that may have unforeseen consequences on ecosystems and human societies. The principles of precautionary measures and intergenerational equity are key ethical constructs that resonate in the debate over adoption and regulation of such technologies.

Beyond these, there is the philosophical debate of anthropocentrism versus eco-centrism in environmental ethics. Should humans be regarded as the central concern of the planet (anthropocentrism), or should nature be valued for its own sake, independent of its utility to humans (eco-centrism)? This difference in worldview profoundly affects how we carve our policies and practice sustainability.

When decisions are to be made, plurality in values can lead to conflicts. If different stakeholders hold divergent views on what constitutes "ethical," the path to consensus becomes a labyrinthine journey. For policymakers, threading the needle between contrasting ethical frameworks is as daunting as it is necessary, for responsible stewardship of the Earth depends on it.

It is the responsibility of those in power to make decisions that are not only scientifically sound but morally robust as well and to foster dialogues to reconcile competing interests and values. The involvement of Indigenous knowledge and community voices ensures diverse perspectives are married into a cohesive sustainability ethic, aligning policy with the deep-seated values of the global tapestry of cultures and communities.

In conclusion, the ethical dilemmas in environmental decision-making are knotty and numerous, demanding a level of sophistication and thoughtfulness that can sometimes seem daunting. Yet, it is precisely in navigating these dilemmas that we can demonstrate our commitment to justice, stewardship, and the greater good. Vigilance and reflection must be our guides as we strive to make decisions that honor not only the Earth's abundance, but also its intrinsic worth. This will allow us to sow the seeds for a future marked by sustainability and equity.

Life in the Anthropocene: Human Footprints

As we delve further into the Anthropocene, the current geological epoch, it's clear that human activity has altered our planet on an unprecedented scale. The Anthropocene is marked by the noticeable impact humans have had on Earth's geology and ecosystems, including, but not limited to, significant alterations to the climate, biodiversity, and natural resources. Understanding this impact is vital as it shapes the very fabric of our existence and challenges us to rethink our role within the broader ecological context.

The onset of the Industrial Revolution marked a pivotal moment in human history, bringing about dramatic changes in technology, economics, and society. However, industrialization also brought a surge in resource consumption and environmental degradation. The long-lasting effects of this period draw us into a reflection on the sustainability of our progress and push us to investigate the balance between the benefits of industrialization and the health of our planet.

Our "carbon footprint," a term now embedded in environmental dialogue, reflects the summation of greenhouse gases we emit, both directly and indirectly. This footprint has expanded so significantly that it is reshaping the atmosphere, influencing climate patterns, and threatening the balance of ecosystems worldwide. The stark reality is that climate change is not merely an environmental concern; it is a comprehensive challenge that impacts food security, water resources, health, and the global economy.

The biodiversity of Earth is suffering a parallel fate. The current rate of species extinction—driven by habitat destruction, pollution, overfishing, and climate change—is estimated to be 1,000 times higher than before human influence. It is not just the loss of individual species that is alarming; it is the unraveling of the complex web of life, which undermines the resilience and functionality of ecosystems.

Water scarcity is another facet of the human footprint, one that casts a shadow over our future. Freshwater resources are becoming increasingly stressed as populations grow and climate change alters hydrological cycles. This scarcity poses profound implications for human health, agricultural productivity, and energy generation, underscoring the need for sustainable water management.

As our cities expand, so does our environmental footprint. Urban areas consume over two-thirds of the world's energy and account for more than 70% of global CO_2 emissions. The urban sprawl and the consequent demands placed on transport, construction, and energy systems require a rethinking of city planning and infrastructure to mitigate the effects of such dense human habitation.

The ecological footprints of agriculture and food production are equally troubling. Intensive farming practices erode soils, diminish genetic diversity in crops and livestock, pollute water systems with runoff, and contribute to greenhouse gas emissions. Transforming our agricultural systems to support sustainable practices is critical for the health of our ecosystems and the security of our food supply.

Furthermore, the waste generated by modern society is a tangible manifestation of our ecological footprint. Single-use plastics, e-waste, and other pollutants do not simply disappear. They often find their way into our oceans and landscapes, causing harm to wildlife and entering our food chain. Sustainable waste management, including the circular economy, presents an opportunity to reduce this footprint and create more closed-loop systems that mimic natural cycles.

Our energy consumption is yet another aspect of our ecological footprint that calls for urgent action. Most global energy still comes from fossil fuels, with renewable energy sources making up a much smaller proportion of the mix. The transition to renewable energy is not just about reducing emissions; it's about securing an energy future that is both sustainable and resilient to fluctuations in resource availability.

To address the challenges of the Anthropocene, we need interdisciplinary and cross-sectoral solutions that recognize the interconnected nature of these issues. This means designing policies that factor in ecological, economic, and social dimensions and employing a nexus approach to managing vital resources like water, food, and energy in concert rather than in isolation.

One of the promising pathways forward in mitigating human footprints is the concept of ecosystem services. By valuing the benefits provided by ecosystems, from pollination to carbon sequestration, we can better integrate natural capital into economic decision-making and create incentives for conservation.

Another avenue lies in adopting a cradle-to-cradle approach in product design and manufacturing. This philosophy promotes the creation of products with multiple life cycles that are, ideally, fully recyclable or biodegradable. Such a shift would not only minimize waste but could also spur innovation and a better alignment of industry with ecological principles.

Education and public awareness are essential components of changing the trajectory of the Anthropocene. Instilling a sense of stewardship and an understanding of ecological principles from a young age can empower future generations to live more sustainably and to demand more from their governments and businesses.

Ultimately, the narrative of the Anthropocene is still being written. While our footprints have been heavy, our capacity for change is immense. The transformative steps we take now can lead to a future in which humanity thrives in harmony with nature, perpetuating a legacy of stewardship and resilience for the Earth we share.

The Anthropocene is our wake-up call. The human footprints etched upon the Earth's surface are deep, but they need not be indelible. The call to action is clear: We must act thoughtfully and decisively to ensure the Anthropocene is not just an epoch of human impact but one of human transcendence toward sustainable living.

Chapter 3:
A World in Flux: Confronting Climate Realities

As we emerge from the historical narratives in which human ingenuity and its paradoxes shaped our environment, we now transition into a present in which those influences starkly manifest as climate realities. Our world, unnervingly dynamic, confronts us with the unequivocal signs of climatic shifts, which challenge not just the stability of ecosystems, but the very bedrock of human civilization.

Climatic phenomena are not simply numbers on a temperature scale or sea levels on a coastal gauge; they vividly translate to livelihoods upended, cultures at risk, and biodiversity in peril. Accepting this profound truth is fundamental, as is our resolve to engage with it. Armed with the best scientific inquiries that map the intricate web of causations, our exploration of this flux must navigate the interwoven economic, ecological, and social fabrics that shape and are shaped by the climate systems in upheaval.

This chapter illuminates not just the gravity of these challenges, but also the resilience and adaptability innate to humanity and the natural world, providing a compass to steer us toward sustainable solutions that are as creative as they are critical. It is here we herald a call to arms for innovative climate mitigation strategies and a readiness for adaptation, crafting the scaffolding for a more resilient society enabled by political, economic, and technological synergies.

The Climate Conundrum: Unearthing the Truth

As we delve into the fabric of our changing climate, we find ourselves at a crossroads where understanding is paramount. Within this labyrinth of complexities lies the essence of the climate conundrum—a puzzle that demands our utmost attention and scientific rigor. It is here, at this junction, we must ask ourselves critical questions and seek out the unvarnished truth about our planet's climate, eschewing the comfort of simplifications for the stark reality of evidence and facts.

While the phenomena of climate change are being intensely studied, controversies and myths still obscure the public's understanding. It is the duty of scientists, policymakers, and informed citizens alike to differentiate between misinformed skepticism and healthy, critical analysis. In doing so, we reveal the robustness of our scientific methodology that encapsulates decades of data, hypothesis, and hypothesis testing through climatology, paleoclimatology, and Earth systems science.

Climate change is not a mere fluctuation of weather patterns, but rather an alteration of Earth's meteorological rhythms that has slowly been unfolding. It is a result of a matrix of natural variability overlaid with substantial human-induced effects, primarily through the excessive release of greenhouse gases such as carbon dioxide and methane. However, to solely focus on greenhouse gases would be a dissection missing its corpus. Therefore, we also examine land use changes, deforestation, and ocean acidification as intricate players within this conundrum.

To unearth the truth of climate change, we must dig into the historical context of industrialization and its repercussions. The age of coal and oil catalyzed our civilization's progress, but it inadvertently set us on a collision course with the natural world. This historical perspective lays the groundwork for a deeper appreciation of the current climatic shifts we are experiencing.

The science of climate change is robust; the well-established laws of physics and chemistry underpin its fundamentals. Surface temperature records, glacial ice cores, and sediment layers testify to the changes occurring. These indicators, along with ecological shifts and increasingly severe weather events, form a corpus of evidence that can't be ignored.

Our understanding of climate connects deeply to modeling future scenarios, which, while varied in their projections, all indicate a trend toward increasing temperatures and related effects. Mathematical models, despite their complex nuances, remain an indispensable tool in climate science, enabling us to explore the potential consequences of our current trajectory.

Yet, the reality of climate change isn't simply an academic discussion—it's felt by communities around the globe. From small island nations facing existential threats from rising sea levels to arid regions grappling with prolonged droughts, the human face of climate impact is as diverse as it is poignant. The intersection of science and humanity is most palpably felt in these tales of adaptation and survival.

The climate conundrum isn't solely a challenge of identifying signals within the noise; it is also about understanding the disproportionate impacts. Economic disparity, resource distribution, and geopolitical tensions are inseparable from the way climate change is experienced and addressed, making it as much a social issue as a scientific one.

Transcending the technicalities, effective communication of climate realities remains paramount. It's about integrating narratives, data, and the lived experiences of people to create not only awareness, but also empathy. A well-informed public is the backbone of meaningful climate action, and education is a catalyst for such a transformative understanding.

Mitigating climate change is a multifaceted endeavor involving technological innovation, policy reform, and sociocultural shifts. This isn't just about curbing emissions; it's about re-envisioning our energy systems, our cities, and our relationship with nature. We find ourselves not at the end of a narrative but at the beginning of a movement—a renaissance of ecological consciousness.

Adaptation strategies, though varied, share common goals: to reduce vulnerability and increase resilience. They're seen in the form of seawalls guarding against storm surges, agroecological practices preserving soil integrity, and community-led resource management. Adaptation isn't merely about coping; it's about transforming adversity into opportunity.

As we continue to confront the climate conundrum, we must do so in a spirit of collaboration, recognizing that no single discipline, nation, or technology can tackle this alone. It requires an orchestra of efforts—harmonious yet dynamic, diverse yet united toward a common purpose. Such a collective response is the hallmark of our generation's mission to safeguard the planet.

In the end, the journey to unearth the truth of our changing climate is both scientific and profoundly human. It touches on our deepest fears and our highest hopes. It challenges our intellect and stirs our spirit. For within this conundrum lies not just a challenge to be solved, but a call to evolve, to reinvent, and to reimagine a sustainable future for all.

Greenhouse Phenomenon: Pinpointing Causes

The greenhouse phenomenon is a natural and essential process that maintains the warmth necessary for life on Earth. However, it is the amplification of this effect due to human activities—chiefly the burning of fossil fuels, deforestation, and various industrial processes—that has led to the current crisis of global warming.

The increasing concentration of greenhouse gases, such as carbon dioxide (CO_2), methane (CH_4), nitrous oxide (N_2O), and fluorinated gases, disrupts the delicate balance of Earth's atmosphere. Human-induced emissions are driving up concentrations of these gases at a rate the natural world cannot mitigate on its own.

Forests act as carbon sinks, absorbing CO_2 from the atmosphere during the process of photosynthesis. When these forests are cleared for agriculture or urban development, not only does this carbon sequestration halt, it also releases the stored carbon back into the atmosphere, further exacerbating the greenhouse effect.

The agriculture sector emerges as another significant contributor. The use of synthetic fertilizers leads to increased N_2O emissions, while enteric fermentation in ruminants—predominantly cows raised for dairy and meat—releases substantial quantities of methane.

Furthermore, industrial activities—including the production of cement and leakages from oil and natural gas systems—have a sizable footprint in the release of greenhouse gases. The extraction, refining, distribution, and burning of fossil fuels create a significant portion of greenhouse gas emissions, underscoring a dependency that needs urgent reconsideration for the health of our planet.

Transportation is another area in which fossil fuel dependence maintains a strong grip. From private cars to public transport systems, ships to airplanes, the burning of gasoline, diesel, and aviation fuel contributes significantly to CO_2 emissions.

The role of energy production cannot be overstated, as coal, natural gas, and oil-fired power plants discharge vast amounts of CO_2 into the atmosphere. The intertwining of energy, industry, and daily life illustrates the systemic nature of the challenge that lies before us.

Human settlements and waste management also contribute to this phenomenon. Landfills emit methane as organic waste decomposes anaerobically, while wastewater treatment releases both methane and nitrous oxide.

Urban sprawl and infrastructure development not only require significant energy, but also change land surface properties, which can affect local climates and contribute to regional warming, further underscoring the anthropogenic factors exacerbating the greenhouse effect.

Not to be overlooked is the impact of fluorinated gases, which, although used in much smaller quantities when compared to CO_2, pack a potent punch due to their high global warming potential (GWP).

While natural factors such as volcanic eruptions and solar irradiance still play a part in climate variation, the overwhelming consensus from the scientific community points to human activity as the dominant force behind the current warming trend.

Our comprehension of the greenhouse phenomenon must be paired with a recognition of its anthropogenic accelerators. It is only through an understanding of the underlying causes that we can hope to devise effective strategies to mitigate this existential challenge.

The key to reshaping our trajectory lies in energy and land use policies. Addressing the greenhouse phenomenon requires a multi-faceted approach that includes transitioning to renewable energy, adopting sustainable agriculture practices, and preserving our forests. To this end, reimagining urban development with sustainability at its core and coupled with innovations in waste management are critical components of the broader battle against climate change.

The imperative for a collective response cannot be overstated. It will take a concerted effort from scientists, policymakers, businesses, and individuals to halt and reverse the current trend. Bridging the science–policy gap, embracing renewable technologies, and nurturing a sustainable ethos within our societies are the stepping stones to ensuring a stable climate for future generations.

Recognizing the gravity of the situation, we must steadfastly commit to act. The climate crisis does not respect geopolitical boundaries; it is a global challenge requiring a unified response. In acknowledging the causes, we forge the first link in the chain of solutions.

Climate Ripple Effects: Economic, Ecological, and Social Dimensions

As we delve into the tangible repercussions of climate change, it becomes evident that the effects are not isolated within environmental bounds but stretch across economic, ecological, and social spectrums. The complexities of these interwoven impacts call for a deeper understanding to uphold the stability of societies and the vitality of nature itself. In the grand narrative of climate realities, the ripple effects form a pattern that is becoming alarmingly more pronounced.

The economic dimensions of climate change are profound and multifaceted. An uptick in extreme weather events, such as hurricanes and wildfires, results in massive financial losses due to property damage, reduced agricultural yields, and disruptions to supply chains. These events can cripple communities and cascade into national markets, causing insurance premiums to skyrocket and investments to tumble. Climate adaptation becomes a costly venture as efforts to fortify infrastructure and insure against potential disasters absorb resources that could have fueled progress in other areas.

The ecological dimensions are equally dire. Climate change disrupts the delicate interspecies relationships that define ecosystems. As temperatures rise, many species that are unable to migrate or adapt fast enough face extinction. This loss in biodiversity not only diminishes the intrinsic value of ecological communities, but also affects human well-being by destabilizing ecosystems that provide essential services such as pollination, water purification, and disease control.

On a social level, climate change acts as a risk multiplier, exacerbating existing inequalities and structural vulnerabilities. Communities that depend heavily on natural resources for their livelihoods are especially at risk. In addition, climate-induced displacements are becoming a harsh reality for many; as sea levels rise and lands become uninhabitable, individuals are forced to migrate, instigating conflicts over resources and worsening the plight of refugees worldwide.

Economic instability brought on by climate change could potentially halt or reverse the progress made in developing nations, undermining efforts to alleviate poverty. The correlation between poverty and vulnerability to climate impacts is irrefutable, as impoverished communities have fewer resources to prepare for and respond to environmental stressors.

The intricate relationship between climate change and food security also presents a significant challenge. Erratic weather patterns and shifting climate zones lead to reduced crop yields and higher incidence of pest and disease outbreaks, threatening the foundation of our global food system.

Health impacts caused by climate change range from the direct, such as heat-related illnesses, to the indirect, such as malnutrition and vector-borne diseases. These health issues carry financial costs in terms of healthcare expenditure and lost labor productivity, further straining economies and social systems.

Moreover, climate change can threaten cultural identity and heritage, as changing landscapes and environments erode the basis for traditions and ways of life for many communities. Indigenous peoples, who often live in harmony with their ancestral lands, face an erosion of culture as climatic shifts upend their traditional knowledge systems and practices.

As we contemplate the future, it's clear that climate change has the potential to disrupt progress on gender equality as well. Women, who make up a significant proportion of the agricultural workforce in many developing countries, are disproportionately affected by climate-related changes that impact food production and water availability.

Addressing the economic, ecological, and social dimensions of climate change calls for an integrative approach. Strategies that bolster economic resilience must simultaneously respect ecological limits and advance social equity. Investments in green technology and sustainable infrastructure can serve the dual purpose of mitigating climate effects while stimulating economic growth.

Adaptation strategies must evolve with ecological dynamics, bearing in mind the interconnectedness of all species. Ecosystem-based adaptation emerges as a promising field, one that can realize the synergies between ecological integrity and human resilience.

At the social front, building community capacity to adapt to climate change is essential. Education and awareness campaigns can empower individuals with the knowledge to tackle climate challenges, while collaborations across various sectors can provide the means for effective adaptation.

Throughout this mosaic of impacts and responses, it's imperative to account for the differentiated experiences of climate change. Equity and justice must form the bedrock of climate policies to ensure the most vulnerable are not left to bear an undue burden.

Addressing the climate crisis is not just about averting ecological collapse or economic downturns; it's about preserving the intricate web that sustains all life on Earth. It requires a profound commitment to stewardship, empathy, and foresight. As we stand at the crossroads of climate realities, the choices we make today will resonate throughout the economic, ecological, and social fabrics of our world.

In pursuing a path forward, we can embrace the potential for innovation and transformation that such challenges present. It's an opportunity to re-envision our relationship with the natural world and each other, fostering a future in which sustainability is not an aspiration but a lived reality.

The discourse on climate change often emphasizes the hazards and hurdles, yet within this narrative, there's room for hope. The very disturbances that threaten our world also galvanize action and creative solutions. We have the capacity to channel the ripple effects of climate change into waves of positive change, steering us toward a resilient and equitable world for generations to come.

Climate Change Headwinds: Political, Economic, and Technological Barriers to Progress

Emerging from the discussions of climate complexities in the preceding chapters, we must address the gales that batter our journey toward climate solutions: political, economic, and technological barriers. These headwinds are the labyrinth to navigate if we are to emerge onto a clear path toward co-creating our sustainable future.

Politically, the challenges are monumental. While science has reached a consensus on the reality of human-induced climate change, political will is scattered across a spectrum of acknowledgment and denial. International efforts, such as the Paris Agreement, while monumental in scope, face hurdles in their implementation. National interests, sovereignty concerns, and geopolitical posturing often eclipse environmental imperatives, leading to slow, or sometimes regressive, policy actions.

Economically, the shift away from fossil fuels, which have been embedded within global industries for over a century, is a colossal undertaking. The existing infrastructure, investments, and market systems resist change due to vested interests and the seismic cost and effort needed to overhaul the energy sector. Additionally, the economic disparities between developed and developing nations introduce strains in climate negotiations in which the latter argue for their right to economic growth.

Technologically, while there has been significant progress in renewable energy, we confront the limitations of storage technology, transmission efficiency, and scalability. Our infrastructure is not yet optimized to handle the whims of wind or the variability of solar generation, and significant investment is required to transition energy systems to accommodate these sources.

Complicating the political landscape are populist movements and the polarization of climate change as an ideological issue. The politicization of climate change stymies meaningful conversation and action. Partisanship erodes the base of shared facts, without which creating robust, adaptable, and widely accepted climate policies becomes ever more challenging.

From an economic perspective, the concept of stranded assets looms large. As we transition to sustainable energy sources, fossil fuel reserves may become virtually worthless—a direct threat to economies and businesses heavily invested in these assets. This potential loss influences many policymakers and corporate leaders to resist or slow transition efforts that are vital for our planet's health.

Technological innovation must also contend with existing regulations and standards designed around old technologies, which create a regulatory lag that hampers the adoption of new, cleaner technologies. In a Catch-22 scenario, new technologies can't become cost-effective without scale, yet they struggle to achieve scale without being cost-effective under current systems.

Additionally, financing for climate solutions is a steep barrier, particularly in nations where other developmental challenges take precedence. Developing countries, facing a range of socioeconomic issues, often find it difficult to allocate funds for climate initiatives or to attract investors in sustainable projects. Furthermore, existing financing mechanisms are seen as inadequate, complex, and sometimes inaccessible for the countries most in need of them.

The role of misinformation cannot be overlooked. The spread of incorrect or misleading information regarding climate science and environmental policies plays a significant role in shaping public perception and can influence political outcomes. This creates an social environment in which unsubstantiated claims can challenge scientific consensus and hamper progress.

Addressing climate change also implies a substantial societal transformation, moving away from consumerism and toward more sustainable living practices. This cultural shift faces resistance rooted in tradition, habit, and the human tendency to prefer short-term gratification over long-term benefits.

While technological advancements can offer solutions, they also bring the potential for unintended environmental impacts and new forms of waste, which must be factored into the equation. For example, producing solar panels and batteries involves processes that are not without environmental issues. Hence, a comprehensive life cycle analysis of new technologies is crucial to ensure they represent a genuine improvement over existing systems.

It's clear political leaders must be bold and willing to look beyond immediate electoral cycles, embrace long-term thinking, and dare to imagine a future that they might not personally behold. It involves transformative legislation, international cooperation, and unwavering commitment to future generations.

Economic systems, likewise, need restructuring toward the principles of a circular economy in which the imperative isn't simply growth but sustainable and equitable growth. In tandem, the financial sector must align with sustainability, incentivizing investments that support long-term environmental health alongside economic prosperity.

From the technological standpoint, we need a renaissance of innovation coupled with a surge in support for research and development focused on sustainability. Only by fast-tracking the development and adoption of technologies that support a sustainable infrastructure can we transcend the current limitations.

In summary, understanding these substantial headwinds is imperative for pacing our actions and expectations. We stand at the precipice of what could either be an era marked by continued discord and environmental degradation or a turning point where humanity rallied against the odds to foster a sustainable world. As pioneers of change, it's crucial that every strategy we employ, every resource we commit, and every innovation we pioneer is focused on navigating these headwinds with precision and unwavering resolve.

Paths to Climate Mitigation: Political, Economic, and Technological Solutions and Innovations

Climate change, once a distant threat, now looms as an imminent crisis, demanding an unprecedented coalition across political borders to ensure a sustainable future. As we've explored earlier in this book, the climate's complexities are profound. Yet, there are paths forward through which we can affect meaningful change. The intertwining threads of politics, economics, and technology underpin these trajectories and offer a blueprint for action.

International cooperation is nothing less than the cornerstone of climate mitigation. The sheer scale of the challenge at hand cannot be understated and it's only through collective action that humanity can hope to steer the course away from disaster. However, such cooperation is fraught with complexity, as nations are guided by differing priorities, levels of development, and vulnerabilities to climate impacts. Nevertheless, the Paris Agreement remains a testament to the possibility of global consensus on climate objectives.

Politically, mitigation strategies require robust policy frameworks that stimulate investment in clean technologies, enforce regulatory standards, and inspire societal shifts toward sustainability. The success of these policies often hinges on their capacity for cross-boundary applicability and adaptability—striving for local relevance while underpinning global climate goals. National governments must step up but so, too, must local jurisdictions to implement policies that resonate within their unique contexts.

Economically, we must incentivize the flow of capital away from fossil fuels and toward sustainable initiatives. This shift necessitates innovation in financial instruments and a rethinking of subsidies that often prop up pollution-heavy industries. Green bonds, carbon pricing, and tax benefits for sustainable practices can turn the tide of investment and demonstrate the compelling economics of clean energy and sustainable industry.

Technological innovation is a dazzling beacon of hope. Advancements in renewable energy, energy storage, carbon capture, and smart infrastructure are already reshaping our world. Yet, for all their promise, these technologies must be deployed equitably. Wealthier nations have a responsibility to aid in transferring know-how and capacity in order to ensure developing regions can leapfrog to cleaner technologies without repeating the carbon-heavy developments of the past.

Renewable energy technology is now often cost-competitive with fossil fuels, a milestone of considerable significance. Scaling up such technologies is key to mitigating climate impacts. Distributed generation systems, microgrids, and enhanced battery storage capacity could revolutionize how we produce and consume energy, particularly in areas where traditional grid infrastructure is lacking or unreliable.

Transportation, a major contributor to greenhouse gases, is on the cusp of transformation. The acceleration of electric vehicle (EV) production and the expansion of public transport infrastructure represent vital steps toward reducing emissions. Encouraging modal shifts from private vehicles to public and non-motorized transport is both a political and cultural challenge, but one that holds immense potential for emission reductions.

In the realms of industry, carbon capture and storage (CCS) technologies offer a transitional means to mitigate emissions. Although not a panacea, these technologies can temporarily reduce the carbon intensity of industries as they pivot toward cleaner processes. However, CCS requires substantial political will and economic backing to bridge the gap between current costs and operation at scale.

Forestry and agriculture hold dual roles as carbon sinks and emission sources. Sustainable land management practices, reforestation efforts, and innovations in agricultural techniques can reduce emissions while enhancing biodiversity and soil health. Political support for these practices, through subsidies and R&D investment, will be vital to their widespread adoption.

An often-overlooked aspect is the need for building resilience in communities, particularly those most vulnerable to climate impacts. Economic planning that includes climate adaptation measures can minimize future losses and preserve developmental gains. This spans from robust infrastructure to ensure protection against extreme weather to social safety nets that aid in rapid recovery post-disaster.

Digital technology also plays an integral role. The IoT, Big Data, and AI are revolutionizing our ability to monitor, analyze, and respond to environmental challenges. Real-time data on air quality, water levels, and crop conditions empower communities to act preemptively against environmental threats through optimizing resource use and improving disaster responses.

Green finance mechanisms must proliferate and evolve to support emerging sustainability-oriented enterprises and models. The growing influence of Environmental, Social, and Governance (ESG) criteria in investment portfolios signals a shift in investor consciousness—one that aligns profitability with planetary stewardship.

The narrative around climate change mitigation is starting to incorporate a broader spectrum of participants. Indigenous knowledge and community-led initiatives are proving invaluable in crafting interventions that are sustainable and culturally appropriate. Political acknowledgment and support of these local-level initiatives can elevate their impact and scalability.

Lastly, the education and empowerment of citizens is paramount. A politically savvy and environmentally literate electorate can hold governments to account, demanding action and prioritizing climate policies. Equipped with the right information and platforms for participation, citizens around the world are a potent force for compelling political and economic actors toward responsible stewardship.

While the scale of climate change can appear daunting, the paths to mitigation are many and within our collective reach. Political, economic, and technological solutions abound. What's required is the courage to commit, the will to act, and the persistence to overcome the barriers that stand in our way. Together, we can architect a world that is not merely survivable but thrives in harmony with the natural systems upon which all life depends.

Ready for Adaptation: Strategies for Resilience

Climate change's relentless churn and consequences on our world are evident and pressing. As the previous sections charted the course of human influence on the planet and dissected the intersecting dominions of ecological, political, and social strata, it's clear the subject of resilience must take center stage. With each passing moment, the imperative for adaptation crystallizes; we are tasked with not only understanding but strategically responding to the unwieldy challenges of climate realities. This section encapsulates the strategies for resilience—a compass for navigation in a capricious climate landscape.

Resilience, as a concept, extends beyond mere survival; it is the insistent and responsive adaptation to changing circumstances that ensures not only persistence but progression. To ready ourselves for a sustainable future, we must embrace systems thinking, an approach that appreciates the intricate web of connections within ecosystems. Recognizing the interdependencies of our natural and human systems allows policymakers, businesses, and communities to formulate multifaceted strategies that buffer against the shocks and stresses climate change induces.

One such strategy hinges on bolstering ecosystem services—the natural processes and functions that support human well-being. For example, by protecting and restoring wetlands, we not only conserve biodiversity, but also create natural barriers to sea level rise and storm surges. Similarly, urban greening initiatives can mitigate heat island effects, reduce energy demand, and enhance the livability of cities amidst rising temperatures.

Further, fostering biodiversity plays a critical role in ensuring resilience. A diverse genetic pool among plant and animal species equips ecosystems with a better chance to recover from disturbances. Strategies that promote habitat conservation and restoration, alongside those that limit human infringement into wild spaces, are paramount. By preserving the variegated threads in nature's tapestry, we uphold the strength and flexibility of ecological systems to adapt.

On the flip side, resilient communities are those that diversify their socioeconomic bases. Local economies heavily reliant on a single industry or resource find themselves particularly vulnerable to climate perturbations. Diversification, whether through the cultivation of varied agricultural crops or the promotion of assorted economic sectors, distributes risk and provides alternative paths for adaptation when conditions change drastically.

Indeed, community-led adaptation initiatives, which harness local knowledge and participation, have shown tremendous promise. These ground-up efforts, ranging from rainwater harvesting schemes to community solar projects, demonstrate the potency of localized actions in building resilience. They empower individuals and communities and foster an adaptive capacity built on the bedrock of local realities and resourcefulness.

Technology, too, finds its place in the adaptation arsenal. Advances in predictive modeling, for instance, give us tools to foresee climate-induced risks and strategize accordingly. Smart infrastructure that dynamically responds to environmental conditions—from flooding-resilient architecture to drought-resistant water systems—exemplifies how we can engineer our way toward resilience.

From an economic perspective, there is a growing appetite for climate-resilient investing. Financial tools, such as green bonds and resilience bonds, not only channel capital toward adaptation projects, but also incentivize the private sector to invest in sustainable infrastructure. Risk assessment models increasingly incorporate long-term climate scenarios, reshaping investment landscapes to favor resilience.

Policy frameworks are instrumental in scaling up adaptation efforts. Mainstreaming climate resilience into development planning, setting stringent building codes, and upgrading zoning laws to reflect future climate projections are all policy levers that can systematically entrench resilience into the societal fabric. Moreover, the interconnectivity of policies, from transportation to agriculture, must be aligned to fortify comprehensive adaptive capacity.

Educational initiatives play their part in priming the mindset of current and future generations. By embedding sustainability and adaptation into curricula, we can cultivate an ethos of stewardship and innovation. Knowledge dissemination stands as a foundational pillar for creating a populace that is informed, engaged, and poised to act in the face of climatic shifts.

Collaboration cannot be overstated when we talk about resilience. Multilateral efforts, spanning across borders and sectors, harness a collective potency. No single entity or nation can turn the tide alone; it is the coalition of forces—international bodies, governments, civil society, and the private sector—that can muster the robust and synchronized response requisite for true resilience.

Finally, acknowledging indeterminacy and embracing a degree of flexibility in adaptation planning can keep systems agile. Scenario planning and adaptive management approaches allow for responsive alterations based on real-time feedback and changing conditions. This iterative process acknowledges that as we increase our understanding of climate impacts, our strategies must evolve correspondingly.

As we stand at this precipice, looking out over a landscape both scarred and shaped by our own hand, there is a palpable sense that our choices, strategies, and actions in this moment are pivotal. We wield the lessons from our past and the tools crafted from our knowledge to endeavor forward, not only to survive but to thrive in a world replete with both challenge and opportunity.

In the end, resilience is as much about the strength to withstand as it is about the wisdom to transform. It's the synthesis of anticipation and action, a dance with dynamic systems in which our adaptability defines our continuity. As we grasp the threads of the resilience strategies outlined, we are knitting together a resilient future—one in which humanity and the planet coexist in a mutually sustaining embrace.

Chapter 4:
The Renewable Revolution: Harnessing Energy

As we turn the page from the visceral recognition of climate realities, we arrive at an empowering epoch—the Renewable Revolution. This chapter delves into the very heart of sustainable energy, examining its current dynamics and the strides we are making toward a paradigm in which energy not only empowers but heals.

We stand on the brink of a transformative era, one in which the boundless vigor of the sun, the steadfast force of the wind, and the bountiful flows of our waters are being harnessed with ever-increasing efficiency and ingenuity. These renewable resources, once viewed as alternatives, are rapidly becoming the mainstay of our energy landscape, promising a future in which clean power is no longer merely a lofty goal but the baseline for all societal endeavors.

In recognizing the innate potential of these clean energies, we are tasked with the critical responsibility of fostering a future that can sustain not just the generation of power but the vitality of our planet and the complex webs of life it supports. The Renewable Revolution is not just about electricity; it's about the re-electrification of the human spirit and our commitment to the flourishing of life in all its myriad forms.

The Shift to Sustainable Energy: Current Dynamics

As we chart the course of our energy future, we must acknowledge the profound shift that is occurring in the field of sustainable energy. The landscape of renewable energy is swiftly changing and reshaping the traditional foundations that have long upheld our energy needs. Solar and wind power, once considered peripheral additions to the energy mix, have transformed into central pillars of our power generation infrastructure. This dynamic shift is a testament to how innovation, driven by the necessity to confront climate change, is revolutionizing the energy sector.

In this fluid environment, the expansion of renewables is both a response to and a catalyst for the further reduction of greenhouse gases. The intertwining issues of climate change, population growth, and the ever-increasing demand for electricity have galvanized a global movement toward sustainable energy sources. The traditional reliance on fossil fuels is gradually being phased out as the production costs of clean energy technologies plummet and their efficiency soars.

Market dynamics increasingly favor renewable energy investments, displaying an emerging preference that echoes both environmental and economic sensibilities. The economics of clean energy have shifted favorably over the past decade, rendering renewables not only environmentally imperative but fiscally responsible choices for many governments and private entities. This fiscal shift is a pivotal moment in the history of energy production and consumption; it marks the beginning of the end of the fossil fuel era.

Technology has played a pivotal role in this evolution. Advances in battery storage, smart grid technology, and energy efficiency measures have enhanced the adaptability of renewable energy systems. The integration of distributed energy resources has further democratized energy, empowering individuals and communities to produce and manage their power supply—a stark contrast to the historically centralized model of energy distribution.

Political will, although varied across regions, is also fueling the shift toward sustainable energy. Policies and regulations that incentivize clean energy production and consumption have begun to alter energy portfolios on a national scale. Initiatives such as carbon pricing, renewable energy mandates, and subsidies for technology research and development are accelerating the transition away from carbon-intensive energy sources.

The corporate sector's role in this paradigm shift cannot be overstated. Many of the world's largest companies are committing to renewable energy, recognizing not just the moral imperative, but also the long-term stability and potential savings associated with sustainable practices. Renewable energy has become a key aspect of corporate social responsibility, risk management, and brand reputation.

As we witness the decommissioning of traditional fossil-based power plants, a compelling narrative unfolds—the narrative of a global society progressively eschewing the combustible engines of the past in favor of the infinite and harnessed breezes and rays of the future. It has become increasingly clear that sustainable energy is no passing trend; it is a profound societal shift with deep ramifications for our collective future.

International cooperation and knowledge sharing have become imperative in disseminating sustainable energy technologies. Global organizations and alliances have arisen as facilitators for this sharing of best practices and strategies, enabling even the most remote areas to access reliable, clean, and affordable energy. This spirit of collaboration is a silver lining, dispelling the shadows of competition and protectionist policies that could hamper our progress toward a sustainable future.

Yet, the transition is not without its challenges. Intermittency issues inherent to wind and solar energy production require innovative solutions for energy storage and grid management. As renewable penetration increases, grid stability and energy security become paramount concerns that require novel approaches and sustained investments.

The reshaping of the energy sector also raises significant questions about the fate of communities tied to the traditional fossil fuel economy. A just transition that considers the livelihoods of these communities, offering retraining and alternative employment opportunities, is essential for the broad acceptance and success of this energy revolution.

In tandem with the technical and market progress, the role of public sentiment and socio-cultural engagement regarding sustainable energy is becoming ever clearer. Clean energy initiatives are significantly bolstered by a society that values and understands the importance of such a transition. This understanding ensures proper public support, community engagement, and consumer behavior aligned with sustainability goals.

Also, advances in energy efficiency have given rise to new building standards and retrofits that significantly reduce energy demands, pairing naturally with renewable energy advancements. The concept of net-zero buildings is becoming not just achievable but increasingly commonplace, signifying a culture that integrates sustainability into the very fabric of our living and working spaces.

Finally, the educational sphere has a crucial role to play in informing and empowering future generations concerning sustainable energy. Bringing these concepts into classrooms and learning spaces ensures the Renewable Revolution is not just about technology and policy but about nurturing an informed citizenry ready to participate in and drive forward the sustainable endeavors of tomorrow.

In conclusion, the current dynamics of sustainable energy presents a vibrant and constantly evolving panorama. It signifies a collective awakening to the opportunities and imperatives of our time—a period marked by technological brilliance fused with a newfound respect for the natural systems that sustain us. It is a revolution not just of energy sources but of mindsets, demonstrating the boundless potential for positive change when human ingenuity aligns with ecological imperatives.

Renewable Energy Spectrum: Analyzing Various Sources

The dawn of the Renewable Revolution signals a transformative shift in how we harness energy to fuel our civilizations. At the heart of this transformation is a spectrum of renewable energy sources, each with its own unique characteristics, potentials, and challenges. As we delve into this spectrum, we must critically evaluate the salient features that distinguish each source, accord mindful consideration to their environmental impacts, and assess their role in a sustainable energy portfolio.

Solar energy, radiant light and heat from the sun, stands as a cornerstone of renewable resources. Its abundance and ubiquity render it one of the most promising clean energy sources. Advances in photovoltaic technology have dramatically increased the efficiency of solar panels, and as a result, costs have plummeted. Large-scale solar farms and residential installations alike contribute to a decentralized energy grid, empowering communities to produce their own electricity and diminish reliance on fossil fuels.

Wind power harnesses the kinetic energy of air in motion to generate electricity. This energy source has witnessed a renaissance in recent years, with turbines growing ever more powerful and efficient. Onshore and offshore wind farms are proliferating at a brisk pace, buoyed by improving technology and increasing cost-competitiveness. Offshore wind, in particular, offers higher and more consistent wind speeds, substantially increasing potential energy yields.

Hydropower, a veteran in the realm of renewable sources, utilizes the energy of moving water to produce electricity. Historically, large dams have dominated this field, offering a dual purpose of power generation and water storage. However, the ecological and social repercussions of large dams, such as habitat disruption and community displacement, have sparked a shift toward smaller, run-of-the-river projects that aim to minimize such adverse effects.

Geothermal energy draws from the Earth's internal heat. Areas with high tectonic activity can harness steam and hot water from beneath the Earth's crust to generate electricity and provide district heating. The base-load and small footprint properties of geothermal power stations add immense value to renewable grids, although exploration and drilling pose certain environmental risks and geological limitations.

Biomass, which includes organic material such as wood, agricultural residues, and even municipal waste, can be converted into energy forms like biogas and biofuels. While offering a renewable option, biomass must be managed sustainably to avoid deforestation and soil degradation and to ensure energy crops do not compete with food production for land use.

Ocean energy—encompassing tidal, wave, and ocean thermal energy conversion—opens a new frontier in renewable sources. The immense power of the world's oceans could be harnessed to provide a substantial portion of global needs, but these technologies are still in relatively embryonic stages, grappling with technical challenges and high costs.

An often-understated source of renewable energy is that of human and animal muscle power. While not scalable to power modern cities, these small-scale, decentralized energy solutions are integral in remote and underdeveloped regions where they provide critical energy services and should not be overlooked in discussions of sustainable energy solutions.

While evaluating these varied sources, it's vital to consider the energy storage solutions that are key to addressing the intermittent nature of renewables such as solar and wind. Battery technology, pumped hydro storage, and even emerging technologies like hydrogen fuel cells are pivotal in ensuring a steady and reliable energy supply.

Transitioning toward renewable sources also necessitates a revision of energy infrastructures. Intelligent power grids, or "smart grids," that integrate storage and efficiency measures are required to optimize the delivery and use of this fluctuating energy supply. Furthermore, upgrading transmission lines, enhancing grid management systems, and embracing digitalization can accommodate the distributed generation paradigm.

Policy frameworks play an essential role in the Renewable Revolution. Subsidies, tax incentives, and regulatory mandates such as renewable portfolio standards encourage investment and technology advancement, leveling the economic playing field with fossil fuels. Such support is crucial during the nascent stages of technology development until economies of scale and innovation drive down costs.

From an environmental standpoint, renewables present a stark contrast to fossil fuels. Decarbonizing the power sector is a monumental step toward mitigating the impacts of climate change. Moreover, renewables typically consume less water, reduce air pollution, and offer a benign counterpoint to the ecologically destructive practices of coal, oil, and natural gas extraction.

It's important to acknowledge that no energy source is entirely benign. Life cycle assessments—considering factors like material extraction, manufacturing energy, and end-of-life disposal—are needed to fully comprehend the environmental footprint of renewable technologies. Although significantly less impactful than fossil fuels, renewables must strive for continuous environmental responsibility.

The future of energy is a mosaic of renewable options tailored to regional potentials, needs, and environmental concerns. Hybrid systems that combine two or more renewable sources can capitalize on their complementary strengths. For instance, a solar-wind hybrid can smooth energy production profiles and counterbalance their respective intermittency issues.

In summary, the renewable energy spectrum is diverse and rich with potential. By embracing this multitude of options, aligning them with smart policies, and pioneering innovative technologies, we can set forth on a trail toward a future that shines with the promise of sustainability, resilience, and harmony with the natural world.

The analysis of renewable energy sources is a testament to human ingenuity's capacity to imagine and manifest a future in which energy is both abundant and aligns with Earth's rhythms. It's a narrative of hope, charting a course on which we can weave a tapestry of technologies that mirrors the very essence of life's diversity and interconnectedness.

Future Energy Landscapes: Potential and Visions

As our journey through the Renewable Revolution unfolds, we gaze into the horizon of future energy landscapes with grounded optimism and a vision enlivened by the burgeoning transformation. We stand at the cusp of an evolving energy paradigm, one that is increasingly decentralized, digitized, and democratized. It's a future that promises sustainability as its cornerstone and upends traditional notions of how we generate, distribute, and consume energy.

In this potential-laden vista, renewable energy sources such as solar, wind, hydro, and geothermal play leading roles, supported by an ensemble cast of transformative technologies. Energy storage systems advance by leaps and bounds, eliminating one of the most persistent limitations to green power—intermittency and unreliability during non-generating periods. Innovations in battery technologies and energy capture methods, such as pumped hydro storage or compressed air energy storage, offer robust solutions for a consistent energy supply.

Smart grid technologies, enabled by the Internet of Things (IoT) and Artificial Intelligence (AI), intelligently manage supply and demand, optimize energy use, and reduce waste. These sophisticated grids can integrate various renewable sources, balance the load by recognizing usage patterns, and deploy energy efficiently across vast networks. This interconnected web of generation, storage, and intelligent distribution is the backbone of a resilient future energy landscape.

The democratization of energy production is another transformative vision. Solar panels and small-scale wind turbines will empower individuals and communities to become producers—not just consumers—of electricity. Community-shared solar and wind farms can distribute the benefits of renewable energy more equitably, creating opportunities for economic growth within local areas and addressing energy poverty.

With the rise of electric vehicles (EVs), the transportation sector—as a significant consumer of fossil fuels—will undergo a profound transition.

Electric mobility is forecasted to intersect with renewable energy generation, allowing vehicles to operate as mobile energy storage units that can feed power back into the grid when needed, creating a symbiotic relationship between the transportation and energy sectors.

In envisioning this promising future energy scenario, we also imagine advancements in less prevalent sources like wave and tidal energy. Harnessing the power of the oceans has the potential to add significantly to the renewable energy mix, given the vast and untapped energy our seas possess.

Hydrogen, emerging as the wild card in the energy deck, holds promise as a clean fuel source. Green hydrogen produced from renewable energy sources—as opposed to traditional carbon-intensive methods—can offer a high-energy, zero-emission fuel alternative for industries in which electrification is challenging, such as heavy transport and manufacturing.

Emerging energy landscapes also reimagine buildings as energy-positive structures that generate more power than they consume. With innovations in materials science, buildings will be equipped with photovoltaic glass and advanced insulation, reducing energy needs while contributing to the grid—effectively turning our living spaces into power plants.

However, this vision isn't just about electricity and hardware; it's also about software—policy frameworks, market mechanisms, and incentive structures. Progressive policies such as feed-in tariffs, renewable portfolio standards, and carbon pricing will be fundamental in driving the adoption of renewable technologies and encouraging investment in clean energy innovations.

Equally important are international partnerships and collaborations that transcend boundaries. Climate change and energy are global challenges that require commitment from every nation—developed and developing alike. Technology transfer and financing mechanisms to support renewable ventures in less-affluent regions will be pivotal in achieving universal energy access and an equitable energy transition.

The visions laid out here aren't merely idealistic dreams; they are within our grasp. Investment in renewable energy sources has been steadily increasing over the years, with a notable surge in the past decade. Global renewable energy investment outpaced that in fossil fuels, reaffirming the confidence of investors in the long-term viability and necessity of the transition.

As we paint this portrait of the future, we are reminded that every brushstroke matters—small acts of innovation, policy decisions, and personal choices all contribute to the larger canvas. There will be technical challenges, financial obstacles, and socio-political barriers, but the trajectory is clear: The Renewable Revolution is underway, unstoppable in its march toward a sustainable and energy-abundant future.

In this vibrant and verdant future, energy is not a source of conflict but a conduit for cooperation, not a privilege but a right, and not a cause for environmental degradation but a champion of ecological harmony. This is the future we envision—a future in which energy sustains not just our machines, but our spirits; not just our economies, but our ethos; not just our lives, but all life.

As this book proceeds, we will not stray into the granular details of renewable technologies or the intricacies of policy instruments, for they deserve their due examination. Instead, we focus on the broad strokes of possibility, the sweeping potential of a new energy canvas, on which every nation, community, and individual can leave their indelible mark.

Chapter 5:
The Waters of Life: Quenching a Thirsty World

The urgent need to preserve and enhance our planet's water resources becomes starkly apparent as we unveil "The Waters of Life: Quenching a Thirsty World." Throughout human history, civilizations have flourished where water is abundant and faced demise when it becomes scarce. Today's world, with its accelerating climate crises and burgeoning populations, is demanding innovative solutions for water conservation and management that were scarcely imagined by previous generations.

In this chapter, we delve into the intricate balance between the sustenance provided by our water systems and the ever-growing demands placed upon them. We'll explore how each drop from clean, flowing rivers to vast, still aquifers is vital to our existence and must be managed with an unwavering commitment to sustainability. Challenges such as scarcity, urbanization, and the vast energy requirements of water purification loom large. As we confront these issues, our narrative will reveal a tapestry of collaborative efforts from action-oriented communities, vigilant governments, and forward-thinking businesses. Together, they epitomize the spirit of water stewardship: preserving this life-giving resource for generations to come.

The Bedrock of Existence: Water in Sustainability

At the core of our striving toward a sustainable future lies a resource so fundamental to life that its importance can hardly be overstated: water. It not merely satisfies our thirst; it sustains ecosystems, nourishes agricultural endeavors, powers industries, and supports the intricate biological processes that maintain the delicate balance of the biosphere. Water's role in sustainability extends far beyond its immediate uses; it is the very bedrock upon which resilient societies are built and maintained.

As we address the resource challenges of the twenty-first century, water assumes a central role in our collective vision for a sustainable world. Efforts to manage and protect this critical resource are entwined with strategies to address climate change, energy conservation, and equitable access. The strategic utilization and preservation of water is not simply about survival; it is directly linked to enhancing the quality of life for all, now and into the future.

Sustainability crusades often focus on renewable energy or waste reduction, but water is perhaps more pressing. Global freshwater reserves are finite, with less than 1% of the world's water readily accessible for direct human use. Water's pivotal position in sustainability is underscored by its scarcity and the growing demand from both population growth and economic development.

The noted economic disparities in water accessibility paint a picture of a world divided by water wealth. Regions abundant in freshwater resources can afford the luxury of diverting this wealth for agriculture, industry, and municipal use. In stark contrast, others face chronic scarcity. The lack of water in these areas impedes economic growth, threatens food security, and gives rise to political conflict.

Clean, fresh water is not only a matter of human welfare, but also a cornerstone for biodiversity and ecological health. Wetlands, rivers, lakes, and other aquatic systems depend on the quality and quantity of the incoming water flow. The ripple effect of declining water quality impacts not just humans but countless other species that rely on these habitats for survival.

To safeguard this vital resource, an integrative approach that encompasses pollution control, demand management, resource allocation, and habitat conservation is paramount. Moreover, the integration of water sustainability into urban planning and building design is a testament to the innovation possible in water stewardship.

Examining agriculture, which accounts for approximately 70% of freshwater withdrawals globally, highlights water's significance in sustainability. This sector carries enormous potential for water-saving innovations such as drip irrigation and sustainable cropping practices. Scaling up such strategies can significantly impact sustainability efforts.

In an industrial context, water is often relegated to a background role, yet its management can profoundly influence efficiencies and impact reduction. Industries are discovering that water conservation and reuse can drive cost savings and environmental benefits equally, creating a compelling case for integrating water sustainability into their operational philosophy.

When considering energy production, the water-energy nexus encapsulates the interdependencies between water use and energy consumption. Hydroelectric power, fracking, and coolant systems for conventional power plants are examples where water use can't be ignored. Sustainable energy solutions must, therefore, consider water conservation at their core.

Climate change further complicates the water narrative. Changing weather patterns, sea level rise, and temperature variability all influence the hydrological cycle, affecting water availability, sanitation, and the natural systems sustained by water. The intersection of climate resilience and water resource management is a crossroad of great urgency.

Regarding policy, integrated water resource management (IWRM) has emerged as a paradigm that recognizes the interconnected nature of water systems across political and geographic boundaries. It promotes coordinated development and management of water, land, and related resources to maximize economic and social well-being in an equitable manner without compromising the sustainability of vital ecosystems.

Tapping into technology, we find it as an aid in monitoring water quality, detecting leaks in urban infrastructure, enhancing desalination processes, and predicting water-related disasters. These innovations offer a pathway to better water management, which is essential for achieving sustainability goals. This is where modern technology partners with timeless natural processes to secure our water future.

Addressing water challenges cannot simply be a top-down effort; it requires community involvement at all levels. Water conservation education, grassroots activism, and public participation in managing local water resources are as vital as governmental and international agreements. It's in these localized efforts that the principles of sustainability find their deepest roots and their most tangible expressions.

Ultimately, the essence of water in sustainability is about harmonizing our needs with those of the planet. It involves recognizing water as a shared resource that requires equitable allocation, judicious use, and vigilant protection. Our collective actions in preserving this precious resource are testament to our commitment to a sustainable and just world for all generations to come.

As we tread the path toward a sustainable world, let us always be cognizant of water's role as the lifeblood of our ecosystems and societies. We must cherish this resource with the reverence it deserves, acknowledging that water's fate is indelibly linked to our own future. For without it, sustainability is but a desert mirage—alluring yet ultimately unattainable.

Ripples of Influence: The Value of Clean Water

The indispensable role of clean water in sustainability cannot be understated. It is the elixir of life, more precious than any commodity. In the context of creating a resilient and nurturing environment, the value of clean water resonates across ecosystems, economies, and societies. Access to potable water is not just a basic human need—it's a critical factor that shapes the health of our planet and its inhabitants.

Clean water is a cornerstone for public health. Waterborne diseases claim the lives of millions every year, a stark reminder that cleanliness equals survival. Unsanitary water sources breed pathogens that lead to diarrheal sickness, one of the leading causes of death in children under five. The effects of clean water ripple beyond just health; they extend to socioeconomic implications. When communities gain access to clean water, the incidence of disease plummets, leading to fewer missed school days and more productive work hours.

From an ecological perspective, clean waterways are essential to biodiversity. Aquatic habitats support a wide array of species and are integral to the overall health of ecosystems. Polluted water not only harms the organisms that live in these habitats, but also affects those that drink from them, including terrestrial and avian species.

Furthermore, water is the lifeblood of agriculture. Irrigating crops with contaminated water can lead to widespread foodborne illnesses and degrade soil quality, impacting food security and farmer livelihoods. Conversely, clean water promotes robust crops, healthier livestock, and by extension, stronger economies.

Industry, too, depends on clean water—not just for manufacturing products, but also for maintaining a brand reputation that increasingly ties to environmental stewardship. Consumers and investors alike are rewarding companies that prioritize sustainable practices, pushing the market toward greater ecological consideration.

Cities and municipalities benefit from clean water through reduced treatment costs and infrastructure stress. When water sources are contaminated, more resources are needed to make them safe. This not only presents an economic burden, but also has a carbon footprint that carries its own set of environmental repercussions.

On a global scale, the pursuit of clean water drives international development and cooperation. Projects that focus on water purification, sanitation, and efficient distribution can be the bedrock of peace and stability in regions where water scarcity could otherwise lead to conflict.

Culture and recreation, too, flourish with the assurance of clean water. Rivers, lakes, and beaches function as communal spaces, sources of inspiration, and playgrounds for the human spirit. They are the settings for traditions, festivals, and leisure activities that enrich lives and cultures.

Yet, even with these widespread benefits, today's water crisis is a clarion call to action. The statistics are startling: nearly one-third of the world population lacks access to safe drinking water, and over half suffer from inadequate sanitation facilities.

Each drop of clean water can trigger a cascade of positive outcomes. For instance, in regions where women and girls are the primary collectors of water, cleaner and closer sources free up time for education and economic activities, leveling the field toward gender equality.

Additionally, clean water is integral to maintaining climate resilience. Healthy wetlands and forests help regulate water cycles and contribute to carbon sequestration. These ecosystems act as natural defenses against extreme weather events, which are increasing due to climate change.

Sustainable water management has the potential to unite sectors and disciplines. It stands as a powerful example of how integrated thinking and cooperative action can address complex challenges. When we align policies, practices, and technologies toward maintaining water purity, we engineer a future in which the environment and humanity can thrive together.

Yet, the path forward is fraught with challenges. Each success in water purification technology, each policy implemented in the name of water stewardship, must be backed by a long-term commitment from all sectors of society. The investments made today in protecting and restoring our water resources will be felt for generations to come.

The narrative around clean water is ultimately one of interconnectedness. It underlines a truth that echoes at the heart of sustainability: The welfare of the planet and the well-being of its people are inseparable. We must foster a future in which clean water flows abundantly, fueling ecosystems, economies, and communities with its life-sustaining properties.

No act of conservation is too small in the context of water. Each effort contributes to a mosaic of actions that uphold our collective responsibility to cherish and protect this vital resource. As stewards of the Earth, we must rise to the occasion, employing every tool at our disposal to ensure clean water remains a universal and enduring legacy.

The Human Watermark: Aquatic Impacts

As we traverse the narrative of our relationship with water, we delve into a profound recognition that our very civilization is irrevocably tied to the water resources of the world. With the furrows of our agricultural endeavors trailing alongside the meandering rivers, and our cities burgeoning at the edges of lakes and coastlines, our reliance on these aquatic systems is unwavering. Yet, the watermark we leave is indelible, raising the critical question: At what point does our dependency translate into destructive dominance?

The hydrological cycle, a sublime journey of water, sustains life. But when we dissect this cycle, we see the scars of human influence. Agriculture, a thirsty guardian of civilization, devours voluminous water reserves. The need to feed a burgeoning population drives us to irrigate expansively, redirecting rivers and draining aquifers. Our mark is not gentle; it shifts ecosystems and alters natural rhythms, undoubtedly undermining our coexistence with the natural world.

Industry, powered by its own unslakable thirst, mines the Earth's waters for process and solution. Rivers and lakes are tapped to cool and cleanse but, often, the return is a blend of thermal and chemical alterations—a cocktail incompatible with life as nature designed it. In the wake of such impacts, we must ask ourselves whether this trajectory can be sustained without irrevocable consequences.

Urban expansion, a testament to our societal complexities, leaves its watermark through surface runoff infused with pollutants, oils, and waste, which transform aquatic habitats into toxic pools. The transformation is not just chemical; it's physical, as concrete banks replace natural shores and the water's edge becomes a stage for human drama rather than ecological harmony.

Climate change, fueled by anthropogenic activities, weaves its narrative through rising sea levels and more extreme weather events, altering habitats and availability of fresh water. As glaciers diminish and seasons skew, old paradigms of water storage and distribution stutter under shifting requirements. The pressing question transpires: Can we adapt swiftly and wisely?

Moving further, we encounter the pharmaceutical imprint. Residues from medications slip through filtration systems, emigrating from our bodies and homes to the communal waters. The long-term impacts on fish and other organisms, subject to our chemical signatures, remain a field ripe for exploration and concern.

Plastic, the hallmark of convenience, flaunts its indestructible nature in oceans and rivers. Microplastics swathe the aquatic environment, entering food chains and presenting an enigmatic challenge with consequences yet to be fully fathomed.

Invasive species, transported by our global trading vessels or released through aquaculture, wrestle with Indigenous lives for space and resources. These intrusive inhabitants—often free from natural predators—can decimate local diversity, remolding ecosystems to their advantage and our detriment.

Acknowledging these human watermarks, we're beckoned to rethink our role. Conservation efforts have steered toward better management practices, guided by the wisdom that healthy water systems are intrinsic to our own health. The implementation of advanced wastewater treatment technologies, stricter regulations on agricultural runoff, and the increased adoption of water-efficient practices across sectors signals a shift in our collective conscience.

Education and engagement are paramount in this journey. Building awareness about the value of water and the myriad of ways in which we impact our aquatic systems encourages more conscientious water stewardship. Promoting citizen science and local water monitoring initiatives empowers communities to take ownership over the health of their waters and advocate for better practices.

Green infrastructure projects that restore natural waterways and create permeable landscapes echo the ethos of returning to nature's blueprints. Mimicking the natural water absorption and filtration systems, they are not merely aesthetic or utilitarian but a reweaving of the relationship between urban life and water cycles.

On the policy frontier, there is a growing demand for the integration of environmental costs in water usage pricing. True-cost accounting can influence more sustainable behavior and fund restoration efforts. Policymakers are also increasingly recognizing the importance of cross-boundary collaboration, acknowledging that water does not adhere to political demarcations.

Through an interdisciplinary approach that bridges scientific understanding and holistic policy frameworks, there's potential for transformative action. Innovations in water-saving technologies, from agriculture to industry, coupled with renewable energy systems that minimize carbon and water footprints, offer promising avenues forward.

Finally, the worldview about our waterscapes we adopt is perhaps the most potent agent of change. When waters are not commoditized but revered as life-sustaining systems from which all living beings spring, our decisions reflect a deeper sense of reverence and responsibility. The human watermark could then emerge as a nuance within the water's own story—a chapter of harmonious existence.

In navigating the fluid narrative of water, the turning tides beckon us to redefine our watermark. As custodians of this blue planet, we bear a profound duty to harmonize with the cycles that sustain all life. Our odes to water must be ones of balance, respect, and ingenuity. The narrative ahead is ours to write. Will they speak of redemption and renewal, or negligence and despair? As a collective, the ripples of our choices stretch far and wide—let us ensure they cleanse, not tarnish, the waters of life.

Challenges to Water Conservation and Purification

As we delve deeper into the essence of sustaining our life-giving waters, it's crucial to confront the myriad of challenges that hinder our efforts in water conservation and purification. Water scarcity isn't just a predicament of arid lands but an impending global crisis that can disrupt the fabric of societies.

While droughts mercilessly throttle entire regions, transforming fertile grounds into barren landscapes, the mammoth energy requirements to treat and deliver water amplify our carbon footprint, contradicting our pursuit of a lower-carbon existence.

Technological advancements, though remarkable, remain inaccessible to many due to high costs or complex maintenance, leaving vast populations dependent on dwindling and contaminated water sources. The rapid urbanization phenomenon challenges existing water infrastructures—often aging and inefficient—struggling to meet burgeoning demands and safeguard water quality.

Rural communities wrestle with a distinctly different set of hardships, from lack of infrastructure to the inequities in water distribution, which are exacerbated for those living in extreme remoteness, whose dire plight is often invisible to policy and decision-makers.

Financial restraints and political apathy can further stifle initiatives, creating a vicious cycle where progress in water conservation and purification is agonizingly slow. As we grapple with these impediments, we must kindle a collective determination to innovate, not only technologically, but also in our governance and community engagement, to navigate through these turbid waters toward a future where every individual has access to the life-sustaining elixir of water.

Water Scarcity and Droughts

Water scarcity and droughts represent one of the most pressing yet underappreciated challenges in our quest for sustainability. As rivers shrink, wells run dry, and landscapes turn brittle under the scorching sun, humanity is confronted with stark reminders of our reliance on the fragile threads of the water cycle. Water scarcity, particularly exacerbated by periods of drastic droughts, is a specter haunting both the prosperity of our communities and the health of our ecosystems.

Droughts, often the result of complex climatic shifts, have become more frequent and intense due to climate change. Arid regions are confronted with the paradox of increasing populations and decreasing water availability. As agricultural sectors gasp for water to sustain crops, the urban sectors also grapple with the imperative to maintain the flow of clean and safe water to burgeoning populations. We find ourselves at a critical juncture where adherence to outdated water-management practices could lead to acute crises, while adaptive, innovative measures may hold the keys to resiliency and endurance.

The human imprint on the water cycle is undeniable, as is the impact of prolonged droughts on water scarcity. The peril of depleted aquifers and reservoirs is not just a theoretical concern—it's materialized in fields lain fallow, in rivers once vibrant now silent, and in communities upended by water shortages. The puzzle posed to us is multifaceted; it requires shrewd governance, community engagement, technological ingenuity, and a commitment to the principled stewardship of our water resources.

To engage water scarcity and drought resilience, we must equally advance our understanding of natural hydrological processes and refine the ways we manage our collective water use. Policies that encourage water conservation, allocate resources with equity, and stimulate innovations in water-saving technologies are essential. Simultaneously, efforts to restore natural landscapes and their ability to retain and manage water can offer a buffer against the crippling effects of droughts. With strategic foresight, investments in infrastructure that either uses water more efficiently or harnesses alternative water sources such as desalination and water recycling can help mitigate water scarcity's gnawing edge.

Crucially, embracing water scarcity and droughts as central tenets of our sustainability endeavors can transform our relationship with water—a shift from that of a mere consumer to that of a thoughtful guardian. This transformation is one that weaves together the essential fibers of ecological understanding, economic efficiency, and social equity to forge a resilient tapestry capable of withstanding the thirst of droughts and the quench of water scarcity. Only through such holistic and anticipatory approaches can we ensure future generations inherit a world where water—our lifeblood—flows sustainably.

Energy Requirements and Carbon Footprint

As we navigate the complexities of water conservation and purification, it's imperative to scrutinize the inherent energy demands and resultant carbon footprint of these processes. Within this framework, the dynamic interplay between energy utilization and carbon emissions emerges as a cardinal aspect of sustainability discussions. We must ask ourselves: How can we mitigate the carbon emissions associated with water treatment infrastructures while ensuring communities have access to clean water?

Water treatment facilities are notorious for their energy-intensive processes, which, regrettably, contribute to the global carbon footprint. Water propulsion through filtration systems, chemical treatments to ensure safety, and the physical infrastructure that supports these processes undeniably require significant amounts of energy. Often relying on fossil fuels, these facilities inadvertently perpetuate the cycle of greenhouse gas emissions, counteracting efforts to reduce climate change impacts.

Recognition of this dilemma has prompted a surge in innovation aimed at the integration of renewable energy sources into water treatment systems. The potential for solar-, wind-, and hydro-powered solutions has gained traction, notably for their dual capacity to slash operational costs and diminish carbon emissions in the long term. Adopting such renewable energy technologies is more than just an environmental imperative; it is also a strategic economic move that aligns with the principles of a circular economy.

Moving forward, consideration must be given to the energy expenditure associated with water transportation. Pipes, pumps, and treatment plants constitute a sprawling network that spans vast distances, tying the carbon footprint of water delivery to the very geography it traverses. Remote communities face a double-edged sword; the requisite infrastructure to provide clean water is accompanied by elevated energy costs and emissions, often resulting in a reliance on diesel generators—a significant source of carbon emissions.

The variable quality of source waters further complicates the task of minimizing the carbon footprint of water conservation and purification. Highly contaminated or saline water bodies necessitate advanced treatment technologies, which, while effective, are accompanied by escalated energy demands. Innovators and researchers stand at the forefront of developing energy-efficient desalination and remediation strategies that promise to lessen the environmental consequences of potable water production.

What's more, our cumulative energy usage attributed to personal water consumption habits cannot be overlooked. The significance of this aspect often dwarfs institutional frameworks, accentuating the individual's responsibility in energy conservation. By introducing water-saving technologies—such as low-flow fixtures and efficient appliances—to our homes and workplaces, we contribute to the grander scheme of reducing the collective energy demand and carbon footprint associated with water use.

Concurrent with these technological approaches, policy frameworks play a crucial role in propelling water conservation and purification practices toward lower carbon footprints. Incentives for utilities that invest in green technologies and penalties for excessive greenhouse gas emissions are pivotal in this transition. It is a dance of regulations and incentives that governments must choreograph with precision to nurture an environment conducive to sustainability.

This interplay between individual choices, technological advancements, policy directives, and infrastructural developments represents a kaleidoscope of actions required to address the energy and carbon concerns in the realm of water sustainability. While the challenge is immense, the dedication to reimagine our water systems as bastions of sustainability rather than sources of emissions holds the promise of carving a path toward a future of balance and responsibility.

Integral to our pursuit of sustainable water practices is aligning strategies with a larger, holistic understanding of the interdependencies that define our ecosystems. The water-energy nexus is a potent reminder that our approach to sustainability cannot be compartmentalized but rather must be as interconnected and dynamic as the systems it seeks to enhance. The journey is undoubtedly complex; however, it's within this complexity that the most transformative opportunities lie.

Technological Limitations

In our crusade to harness technology to serve the Earth's water systems, we acknowledge the mighty rivers of progress, but also the tributaries that run dry. Technology, while a beacon of hope, comes with limitations—stalwart obstacles that we must navigate in our journey. For those dedicated to the craft of water conservation and purification, understanding these technological confines is not just crucial—it is essential for effective planning and innovation.

The very sophistication of modern water treatment technologies can be a double-edged sword. Advanced filtration systems, such as reverse osmosis and nano-filtration, require significant energy input and specialized maintenance. While these systems are paramount in providing clean water, the energy demanded imposes a carbon footprint that can't be ignored—an environmental consideration we grapple with as we strive for sustainability.

Furthermore, scalability poses a considerable challenge. Technologies proven to be effective in laboratory settings or small-scale applications often encounter unforeseen issues when scaled to meet the demands of large populations. The infrastructure required to expand these water-purification technologies in a cost-effective manner isn't always available, especially in regions experiencing rapid urbanization or in remote landscapes where the reach of modernization is yet to be felt.

Monitoring and control systems present another hurdle. Implementing sensors and IoT devices that provide real-time data and automation of water treatment processes demands a level of technical expertise and economic investment that can be daunting. Many communities, especially those in the developing world, struggle to attract and maintain the skilled workforce necessary to manage these intricate systems.

Moreover, the persistence of contaminants that can evade current treatment methodologies is becoming increasingly apparent. Emerging pollutants, such as microplastics and pharmaceutical residues, challenge the capability of existing technologies, and their gradual buildup in the aquatic environment casts a long shadow on our optimism.

Reliability and durability underpin yet another dimension of these limitations. Water purification components are subject to wear and tear, and in regions lacking the resources for regular upkeep and replacements, these system failures can significantly disrupt the provision of clean water. The components' susceptibility to damage from environmental factors, such as extreme weather events linked to climate change, further exacerbates their fragility.

The inherent diversity of water sources complicates technology application. Treatment systems designed for certain water types may not be universally applicable, necessitating customization that hinders the one-size-fits-all solution many seek. As a result, each community must embark on a convoluted process of identifying the technology that aligns with its unique water characteristics—adding cost and complexity.

Not all citizens have equitable access to advanced treatment technologies due to economic disparities. Affluent areas might enjoy the benefits of cutting-edge systems, while economically disadvantaged communities continue to use less-efficient, outdated methods—perpetuating a cycle of inequality in water quality and health outcomes.

As stewards of our blue planet, we are called to not merely acknowledge these technological challenges but to confront them with inventive spirit and collaborative resolve. Overcoming these limitations is not an insurmountable task. Through innovation and continuous research, we can develop technologies that are robust, energy-efficient, scalable, and adaptable to diverse environments. The future of water technology is not a testament to our limitations but to our limitless potential for ingenuity.

Let every challenge ignite a spark of creativity, for the wellspring of human achievement is inexhaustible when we pool our collective energies toward the common good. Our commitment to refining technologies, optimizing energy use, and ensuring equitable access to water treatment is what will ultimately guide us toward a sustainable future—one purified drop at a time.

Urbanization and Water Infrastructure

The relentless march of urbanization is a defining feature of our era. It shoulders the promise of progress, but also often bears the burden of strained water infrastructures with each sprawling metropolis it births. Understanding this dichotomy necessitates a deep dive into the interplay between urban expansion and the life-sustaining systems that provide for our most basic of needs—water.

In cities around the globe, the surge in population density embroils existing water infrastructure under immense pressure, leading to a nexus of challenges. The aged pipes and treatment plants, often exceeding their life expectancy, are simply ill-equipped to cope with the surging demands of a burgeoning population. This is less of a technological failing than a cautionary tale of human shortsightedness in which the foresight needed to accommodate growth was eclipsed by the immediacy of urban development. Moreover, in cities where infrastructure was hastily erected to match the swift pace of growth, quality and sustainability were inevitably compromised.

The ultimatum presented by urbanization is stark: either we innovate or we resign ourselves to a future of water shortages, pollution, and the gratuitous waste of runoff in the torrents of stormy seasons. The sustainable orchestration of cityscapes demands an intricate balance. Where water once freely percolated through the soil, now impermeable concrete diverts it, challenging the very cycles that replenish our aquifers. The shift toward permeable materials and green spaces within urban settings is not merely aesthetic—it is an elemental reclamation of the water cycle itself.

With urban development occurring at breakneck speeds, particularly in emergent economies, the opportunity and need for innovative water-management solutions cannot be overstated. These include, but are not limited to, rainwater harvesting, gray water recycling, and advanced wastewater treatment facilities integrating renewable energy. Adopting such systems could mitigate the burgeoning water demands of cities while preserving the integrity of their water cycles.

Moreover, integrated water resource management (IWRM) presents itself as an imperative framework, uniting various stakeholders in the coordination of land and water management with a focus on the sustainable development of urban ecosystems. Within the IWRM approach, the decentralized water treatment and the co-management of water services empower communities and enhance resilience to water-related stresses. By embedding such inclusive practices, we instill a collective sense of ownership and responsibility toward our most precious resource.

Climate change further compounds the urban water conundrum, bestowing episodes of drought and flood in unpredictable patterns. Our built environments must, therefore, be agile, anticipating and adapting to these hydrological extremes. Investments in infrastructure must extend beyond mere capacity expansion; they must imbue resiliency, championing systems that can withstand, recover, and adapt to the vagaries of a changing climate.

Within the urban context, the synthesis of green infrastructure with traditional water systems is gaining traction. Rain gardens, bioswales, and constructed wetlands don't just beautify neighborhoods—they perform the critical function of managing stormwater, reducing runoff, and recharging local aquifers, acting as natural purifiers in the process.

And yet the bridge between what is technologically possible and what is politically and financially viable is frequently a chasm. Budget constraints, policy gridlocks, and competing interests often sideline the essential upgrades needed for sustainable urban water management. Thus, engaging not only governments and industry but also civil society in the discourse of water infrastructure is vital. Public policy must be echoed by public support and advocacy to pave the way for the essential transformations ahead.

Education and awareness campaigns can provoke a wave of support for such vital investments, inviting not just acceptance but enthusiasm for the developments essential for our continued urban thriving. By empowering citizens with the knowledge of the challenges and potential solutions, we catalyze the collective will needed to invest in sustainable water infrastructure.

Ultimately, as we pave streets and erect skyscrapers into the heavens, our respect and reverence for water must remain foundational in our quest for progress. The cities of tomorrow hinge upon the ingenious management of this life-giving resource. The transformative power of urbanization, when steered with prudence and vision, can forge metropolises that are not merely hives of human endeavor but beacons of sustainability.

Rural Challenges

As we contemplate the mosaic of water conservation and purification, it's imperative not to overlook the rural canvas, which is etched with its unique set of challenges. The discourse on sustainability often pivots around urban centers, but the rural heartlands are just as vital to the tapestry of our environmental endeavors. Rural communities frequently harbor intimate connections with the natural water sources that sustain them yet face myriad obstacles in safeguarding these precious lifelines.

In the outstretched arms of countryside landscapes, the tyranny of distance plays a critical role in water-related woes. Accessibility to cutting-edge treatment facilities or sophisticated distribution networks often falls beyond the grasp of these settlements. Rural dwellers may rely on wells, springs, and surface water, which, while being direct links to nature's bounty, are also vulnerable to contamination from agricultural runoff, inadequate sanitation, and industrial activity.

The technological limitations urban areas can counter with infrastructure and capital investment turn into mountainous trials for rural spaces. The dearth of funding opportunities and the often–higher per capita costs of servicing sparsely populated areas further exasperate the plight. For instance, advanced water-purification processes that mandate substantial energy inputs, complex maintenance, or specialized expertise are not readily transplantable into the rural setting.

Rural challenges are compounded by the nature of the economies typical to these domains. Predominantly agrarian or resource based, rural economies can be intricately tied to practices that compromise water quality, such as conventional farming techniques that may contribute to nutrient pollution via fertilizer and pesticide application. Thus, water protection efforts are not just about provision and purification but about transforming the core practices of rural livelihoods.

The implications of climate change insidiously exacerbate rural water concerns. As rainfall patterns shift and temperatures swing, the hydrological cycle is upended, leading to events like droughts or floods that disproportionately impact rural communities due to their reliance on weather-dependent resources and lack of resilience infrastructure.

Yet, in this portrait of hardship, we must also paint the strokes of resilience and adaptive innovation that rural populations exhibit. They often possess a well of traditional knowledge shaped by generations of interaction with their environment. Harnessing this resource is key to bridging the gap between modern sustainability principles and practices well-suited to the rural setting.

Inclusivity in policymaking is a clarion call we must heed to address rural challenges effectively. Strategies that work for metropolitan areas may not fit the distinct framework of rural life. Flexibility and adaptation, therefore, are paramount; policies need to account for the variability in rural infrastructure, funding, and social dynamics.

Fostering networks of collaboration among rural communities can lead to the sharing of resources, expertise, and support, making each community more robust against the tide of challenges. Cooperative management of watersheds and water systems can allow communities to pool their limited resources for greater collective impact.

The education and empowerment of rural inhabitants to engage in sustainable water practices is of the essence. It requires outreach and education programs tailored to the rural context, perhaps leveraging the school systems, local NGOs, or extension services traditionally used for agricultural education.

Despite the daunting landscape of challenges, moments of ingenuity and perseverance amongst rural folk offer rays of hope. The implementation of rainwater harvesting systems, the revival of ancient water conservation methods like terracing, and the adoption of low-tech water-purification systems showcases the ability of rural communities to adapt and thrive.

Indeed, the successful sustainability narrative in rural areas lies in an empathetic approach that aligns with precisely these sorts of localized, feasible innovations. This entails fostering sustainability within the existing cultural and economic fabrics of rural societies, rather than imposing one-size-fits-all solutions detached from the reality on the ground.

Mobilizing financial resources and investment in rural water systems also signifies a hurdle. But should we pool efforts across government, private sectors, and international development agencies, it is a surmountable one. Incentives for protecting water resources "at the source" by these stakeholders can generate a ripple effect, enhancing the quality and availability of water downstream and further afield.

We stand at the confluence of traditional wisdom and emerging innovation. We must reach across disciplines and meld the hands of farmers, scientists, policymakers, activists, and local citizens to craft integrated water-management strategies that are as diverse and dynamic as the rural landscapes we seek to sustain.

The march toward sustainable water systems in rural realms is a testament to human resilience and ingenuity. It is a journey of challenge, indeed, but also of immense opportunity to craft systems of water stewardship that resonate with the echo of sustainability's beating heart. It is here, beneath wide-open skies and among the murmurs of streams and the rustle of fields, we might rediscover the sanctity of water, essential yet so often overlooked, and chart a course that ensures its bounty for generations to come.

Challenges for Very Remote Communities

As we delve deeper into our discourse, it becomes crucial to turn our lens to the very remote communities, those outposts of humanity that are often overlooked in broad discussions about sustainability. These communities face a unique set of challenges, magnified by their isolation and often compounded by limited resources. Understanding these challenges is vital because each community holds a piece of the puzzle in our collective quest for a sustainable future. In the dance of progress and preservation, the struggles of remote communities strike a poignant chord that resonates with the global imperative for change.

Communication and virtual connectivity, often taken for granted in urban spaces, can be sporadic or non-existent in remote areas. Such isolation not only inhibits the flow of vital information and innovative ideas, but also hinders emergency assistance during times of crisis. This hampers both the region's development and its ability to engage with global sustainability efforts.

Accessibility, both geographical and economic, poses another staggering challenge. With limited physical infrastructure, basic needs and services—including healthcare, education, and even clean water—become luxury commodities. Roads may be rudimentary if they exist at all, making travel arduous and dangerous. The high cost and difficulty of transporting goods translate to a heightened cost of living and an increased carbon footprint for necessary imports.

Energy availability is another profound hurdle. The remoteness often translates into an absence of a reliable energy grid, coercing communities to rely on diesel generators that are both costly and environmentally detrimental. The potential for renewable energy is vast, yet harnessing it requires expertise and scarce investments.

Furthermore, the intimacy of these communities with their environment implies direct exposure to the adverse effects of climate change. These communities often inhabit areas where environmental disasters—such as floods, droughts, and severe storms—are not just possibilities but realities that disrupt lives and livelihoods, undermining their resilience.

Food security is an omnipresent concern, as the remote nature of these habitats leads to reliance on limited local produce and costly transported foodstuffs. The increase in greenhouse emissions from transportation further exacerbates their carbon footprint, nourishing a cycle of unsustainability.

The nuances in the relationship between Indigenous knowledge and modern sustainable practices present both an opportunity and a challenge. While Indigenous wisdom can guide sustainable living, harmonizing it with new technologies and practices is essential for progress, yet often difficult to achieve.

Economic constraints can be stifling as financial resources in remote regions are often scarce. This scarcity hampers the ability to invest in the infrastructure and technology needed to embark on sustainable practices and hinders development initiatives.

Remote communities also face barriers in governance and representation. The distance from political centers means their voices and needs are often marginalized in policymaking processes, leaving their unique challenges unaddressed. Without a seat at the table, the prospects of tailored sustainable solutions are dim.

This milieu of challenges uniquely influences the health of resident populations. The lack of access to adequate healthcare services and infrastructure compounds the aforementioned issues, setting off a domino effect on overall well-being.

One must also consider the psychological impacts of such isolation. The feeling of being left behind in a world marching toward connectivity and integration can engender a sense of abandonment and helplessness, which could undermine local initiatives toward self-sustenance and environmental stewardship.

Education systems in remote communities struggle with resource constraints, leaving a gap in the knowledge necessary for driving innovation and sustainability. The future stewards of these lands need educational nourishment to sow seeds of change that can flourish into sustainable practices.

The dichotomy between maintaining traditional lifestyles and embracing necessary change presents its own set of challenges. Balancing cultural preservation with the inevitable need to adapt to persistent environmental changes is a delicate dance that these communities must perform.

Technological lag due to inadequate infrastructure and funding means very remote communities miss out on innovations that could catalyze their sustainable development. Without these technologies, they lag even further behind the global march toward sustainability.

Within the knowledge of these formidable challenges lies the beckoning of opportunity—the chance to engage with remote communities in a manner that empowers them. By lending ears to their narratives, we can draft a blueprint of support that respects their unique situations and integrates their voices into the chorus calling for sustainability.

It is here, in the hearts of these far-flung communities, we uncover the raw essence of endurance and adaptability. Their plight, their battles with the elements, and their survival strategies serve as a microcosm of the global challenge we face. Integrating their insights into wider sustainability strategies is not just an act of inclusion but a necessity for crafting enduring solutions. After all, sustainability is not solely about technology or urban systems—it's about people, their environments, and the thread that weaves us all into the tapestry of life on this planet.

Financial and Political Barriers

As we delve into the realm of water conservation and purification, it's imperative to confront the nuanced complexities that financial and political landscapes impose. Financial barriers often emerge as sizable impediments, predominantly in regions struggling with economic instability or scarcity of resources. Investment into water infrastructure requires capital—capital that is often unfairly distributed around the globe. Political barriers, meanwhile, are equated with the intricacies of governance and ideology, in which water rights and access can become fiercely contested, and policymaking may be stymied by differing priorities or bureaucratic inertia.

Understanding these barriers necessitates a frank discussion about the allocation of funds and the role of government. Infrastructure projects to improve water conservation and purification systems often demand long-term investments that may not align with political cycles. This misalignment can result in a lack of continuous support, with projects initiated by one administration potentially stalling as another takes office. Furthermore, water infrastructure is not just about pipelines and treatment plants; it's about building resilient communities that can endure the caprices of a changing climate. However, all too often, the urgency of these projects fails to resonate within political agendas focused on short-term gains or re-election bids.

Additionally, corruption and mismanagement can steer precious funds away from water projects, exacerbating financial barriers. When governance is flawed, the ramifications are felt through delayed or defunct projects, denying communities access to the essential resources they direly need. Similarly, political will is an indispensable factor in water management. Regions fraught with political instability or conflict struggle immensely with advancing water conservation because governance systems are either non-functional or engaged in other pressing matters.

At the heart of these barriers lies the macroscopic challenge of balancing economic development with environmental stewardship. Policymakers must be persuaded to reconceptualize water infrastructure not as a cost, but as an investment in sustainable development and public health. The message that must cut through is that sustainable practices in water management are not just acts of ecological righteousness but are foundational to economic resilience and societal well-being. For it's within the droplets of pure, conserved water that the vitality of human progress and ecological harmony coexist.

The task before us is to garner the support required to overcome these financial and political barriers—to advocate for equitable funding structures and to cultivate a political milieu in which water, a source of life, transcends the often-murky waters of politics. It's through informed dialogues and decisive actions that we can shift the tide, ensuring every community, irrespective of its economic standing or its political landscape, has access to the clean, sustainable water it needs. Despite these impediments, our resilience and commitment can clear the path for significant advancements in water conservation and purification, for the sake of all who call this planet home.

Water Stewardship: Public and Private Sector Roles

The essence of sustainability is interwoven with the threads of water stewardship, a concept that binds both the public and the private sectors in one shared agenda: to manage our most critical resource responsibly. As we delve into the roles of various sectors in water management, we must recognize water is the lifeline of our civilizations, ecology, and economies.

The role of public institutions in water stewardship cannot be overstated. Governments are responsible for setting, implementing, and enforcing policies that ensure the availability and quality of water for their citizens, ecosystems, and industries. To accomplish this, they employ a variety of tools, from regulations and tariffs to public education campaigns and subsidies for sustainable water technologies. The ongoing challenge lies in balancing the need for economic development with the urgency of environmental conservation—and always within the confinements of limited resources.

Within the public sector, there's also a dire need for integration and collaboration across different agencies and departments. Water does not abide by man-made boundaries, and, thus, its governance requires a holistic approach. It is imperative for the agencies handling agriculture, environmental protection, urban planning, and energy to work in unison—each appreciating the water-related impacts of their decisions.

On the other side of the spectrum, the private sector assumes a pivotal role in water stewardship through innovation and investments. Corporations, particularly those within industries such as agriculture, manufacturing, and energy, are substantial water users and have a vested interest in guaranteeing the sustainability of this resource. In fact, many companies are realizing water stewardship is not merely a corporate social responsibility initiative but a strategic imperative for long-term viability.

The private sector can spearhead technological advancements that conserve water or improve its quality. For example, the development of water-efficient appliances and industrial processes can have a significant impact on water savings. Companies are also investing in advanced water-treatment technologies that enable recycling and reuse, helping to close the loop on water use within their operations.

Moreover, there is an increasing push for transparency and reporting regarding water usage and sustainability efforts in the private sector. Such practices not only promote accountability, but also foster trust with stakeholders, investors, and consumers who are becoming ever more conscious of environmental impacts.

The impact of partnerships between public and private sectors in water stewardship should not be underestimated. These alliances bring together the regulatory expertise and reach of governments with the innovative prowess and efficiency of businesses. They can be instrumental in tackling large-scale projects, such as modernizing aging water infrastructure, which neither side could manage alone due to financial or operational constraints.

Community involvement is another cornerstone of effective water stewardship. Local communities often have a deep understanding of their water resources and are most directly affected by water-related decisions. Their engagement in water governance—from planning stages to implementation and monitoring—ensures initiatives are tailored to the actual needs and challenges on the ground. Environmental stewardship programs that involve citizens can cultivate a sense of ownership and responsibility toward local water resources.

Educational initiatives and awareness campaigns are vital tools in the public sector's arsenal for promoting water stewardship. They encourage sustainable practices—such as reducing water wastage, protecting waterways from pollution, and supporting water-efficient technologies—among individuals and businesses. These campaigns, when effective, alter public perception and habits, aligning them with sustainability goals.

In recent years, there has been a surge in collaboration on an international scale, with treaties and agreements bringing nations together to address shared water challenges. Transboundary water management poses its own unique set of challenges, yet international cooperation remains crucial for addressing issues such as river pollution and the equitable distribution of shared water resources.

Moreover, the financial and investment community is turning its attention to water risks and sustainability, making it a factor in investment decisions. This trend is giving rise to sustainable financing mechanisms, such as green bonds, which explicitly fund projects that have positive environmental and water-related benefits. These financial instruments can be powerful drivers of change when aligned with clear water stewardship outcomes.

To truly embed water stewardship within the fabric of societies and economies, it must become an integral part of the education system. From an early age, students should be taught about the value of water, the complexities of water systems, and the critical skills needed to manage and conserve this resource sustainably. Such knowledge would equip future generations with the acumen to continue advancing sustainable water-management practices.

The path forward must include the cultivation of shared values centered around water stewardship. This encompasses recognizing the intrinsic value of water beyond its economic uses—acknowledging its role in culture, well-being, and life itself. This paradigm shift is essential for both the public and private sectors to view water not as a commodity but as a shared, precious resource.

In conclusion, water stewardship demands the collective effort of both the public and private sectors. Each role is distinct yet complementary and, together, they form the force necessary to ensure the sustainable management of our most vital resource. As we progress, it's essential to remember every action, policy, and innovation in water stewardship not only addresses an immediate need, but also echoes into the future, shaping the world for generations to come.

Chapter 6:
Oceanic Heritage: Guarding the Marine Commons

After delving into the criticality of freshwater resources, our focus shifts to the vast marine environments that cradle life on our planet. In "Oceanic Heritage: Guarding the Marine Commons," we embark on an exploration of the boundless blue frontier, understanding the immense value oceans hold beyond their shimmering surfaces.

Our marine ecosystems aren't just stunning in their biodiversity; they're also pivotal to global climate regulation and are the wellspring of life-sustaining functions that we can't afford to neglect. Yet, as we peer into the abyss, we're quickly confronted with the stark challenges posed by overfishing, pollution, and acidification, pressing us to defend these commons with cutting-edge conservation strategies and governance. It becomes ever clearer that the fate of the ocean is inextricably linked to our own—prospering only if we recognize its intrinsic value and the need for its urgent protection.

Unraveling new threads of innovation, we'll uncover the transformative potential of Marine Protected Areas (MPAs) and policy frameworks that give life to sustainability's ethos, heralding a beacon of hope amidst turbulent tides. As we navigate through this chapter, every crest and trough will carry the resolute message that the survival of the marine commons isn't just an environmental imperative—it's a legacy we ought to cherish and uphold for the health and continuity of all life on Earth.

Oceans Unveiled: Their Pivotal Role in Our World

The mention of oceans conjures images of vast blue horizons, the pulse of tides, and the chorus of marine life. What is often less apparent is how central these watery expanses are to the well-being of our planet and, by extension, all of humanity. Covering over 70% of the Earth's surface, oceans are immense reservoirs of biodiversity, moderators of climate, and providers of essential resources, framing the very foundation of our existence.

Oceans serve as a colossal heat sink, absorbing heat-trapping gases and storing nearly 50 times more carbon than the atmosphere, playing an indispensable role in the climate system. This vast capacity for heat and carbon absorption provides a buffering effect against climate change, with the deep sea acting as one of the world's largest carbon sinks.

Marine ecosystems, ranging from coral reefs to deep ocean trenches, not only house millions of species—many of which are yet to be discovered—but also support human societies through fisheries, recreation, and cultural significance. The profound biodiversity found under the waves drives innovation in sectors such as medicine and technology while supporting livelihoods of communities both coastal and inland.

Human survival is deeply interwoven with the health of the oceans. They provide a source of nutrition for billions of people, with fish accounting for around one-sixth of the animal protein people consume worldwide. Vital shipping lanes crisscross the briny depths, forming the backbone of global trade and facilitating the movement of goods across continents.

Yet, despite their centrality to life on Earth, oceans face unprecedented threats from overfishing, pollution, habitat destruction, and consequences of climate change such as ocean acidification and warming. Acknowledging their pivotal role in our world isn't just about admiration but about understanding the urgency of conserving these marine commons for future generations.

To fathom the vastness of the seas, consider that the Pacific alone covers a larger area than all the Earth's land combined, while the deepest point in the Mariana Trench plunges over 10,000 meters below the surface—far exceeding the height of Mount Everest. This vastness represents a sanctuary for life, a silent witness to our planetary history, and a vast library of biological and chemical processes yet to be fully understood.

Oceans are the architects of weather and climate, driving rain patterns and temperature gradients that enable life to flourish in diverse ecosystems. The ocean–air exchanges are critical in shaping weather phenomena, from nurturing monsoons that sustain billions to brewing hurricanes that remind us of nature's formidable power.

The importance of oceans extends beyond their tangible offerings. Culturally, they have been revered across civilizations, inspiring literature, art, and religion. Stories of ocean voyages are stories of human curiosity and resilience, a testament to the indomitable spirit that journeys across uncertain waters toward the promise of discovery.

Oceans, as a shared global commons, require cooperative stewardship. They don't adhere to national borders or succumb to partisan politics; their currents and creatures traverse vast distances, indifferent to human divisions. Our conservation efforts, thus, must be equally boundless and inclusive, engaging all sectors of society from policymakers to local communities.

Technology provides a beacon of hope for oceanic conservation— from satellite tracking of illegal fishing to AI-powered monitoring of coral reef health. Yet, technology is not a panacea. It must be wielded with a sense of humility and coupled with traditional ecological knowledge that Indigenous and coastal communities have cultivated over millennia.

Education about oceans can no longer be contemplative; it must be an active, vibrant pursuit. Children splashing along the shoreline should grow up understanding not just the joy of the ocean's embrace, but also the responsibilities that such joys entail—for they are the future custodians of these blue realms.

Sustainable ocean management isn't just an environmental concern—it's an economic imperative. The global ocean economy is valued in the trillions, demonstrating the economic interdependence between human prosperity and ocean health. Investments in marine protection are, in essence, investments in our collective economic future.

The myriad connections between humans and the seas—whether through the air we breathe, the seafood we consume, or the climate on which we rely—form a nexus that underpins life itself. In this connection lies not only our greatest challenges, but also our most profound opportunities for crafting a sustainable future.

As we chart our course through turbulent times, let's not forget the oceans—their waves whisper the history of our world and hold the keys to our sustainable future. In protecting and valuing these marine commons, we unleash the potential of the seas to support a prosperous, resilient, and sustainable planet for all life forms.

We stand at a pivotal point where each drop of effort can ripple out to create waves of change. It's time to dive deep into ocean conservation, restoring the balance in our marine heritage—a treasure trove of biodiversity and a critical ally in the struggle against climate change. Our oceans have unveiled their pivotal role. Now, it's our turn to act, ensuring the oceans can continue to safeguard our world for ages to come.

Economics Beneath the Waves: Ocean Value Unleashed

As we delve further into understanding our planet's interconnected systems, the economics of ocean management prove to be as deep and wide as the oceans themselves. The value encapsulated beneath the waves is not only ecological, but also economic, with a richness that rivals any terrestrial treasure. The bounty of the oceans, if harnessed sustainably, holds keys to unlocking new economic potentials while maintaining the balance of marine ecosystems.

Ocean economies, a term encompassing all economic activities connected with the sea, are monumental. The ocean is a hub for industries such as fishing, shipping, and tourism, which contribute immensely to global economic health. Fisheries alone provide the primary source of protein for billions and generate a turnover of billions of dollars annually. But to fully appreciate the wealth of the oceans, we must look beyond extraction to the oceans' roles in climate regulation, carbon sequestration, and biodiversity support.

The untold worth of the ocean's services to humanity is staggering. Marine ecosystems such mangroves, salt marshes, and seagrass meadows are invaluable carbon sinks, sequestering CO_2 at rates far surpassing terrestrial forests. The protection and restoration of these blue carbon ecosystems are not just environmental imperatives; they are economically sensible strategies for mitigating climate change.

Moreover, the oceans are frontiers for renewable energy, whether through wind, tidal, or wave power, offering alternatives to fossil fuels. The burgeoning field of marine renewable energy has the potential to provide a substantial portion of our energy needs. Harnessing these resources sustainably could drive a new economic wave, create jobs, energize industries, and propel innovation.

Ecotourism is another vibrant source of revenue that underscores the beauty and importance of healthy marine ecosystems. Regions with well-preserved coastlines and rich marine life attract millions of visitors annually, underlining how conservation can dovetail with economic growth. The equation is simple: Protecting our oceans can prove profitable.

Yet, all this is not without challenges. Overfishing, pollution, and habitat destruction have long been the adversaries of the oceans' economic value. Coral reefs, known for their outstanding biodiversity and ecosystem services, face bleaching due to increased sea temperatures. The loss of reefs not only spells disaster for marine life, but also for the economic well-being of communities that rely on them.

Despite these challenges, solutions are on the horizon—ones that integrate economic and environmental objectives. Aquaculture, or fish farming, when practiced responsibly, can relieve pressure on wild fish stocks and provide livelihoods. Innovations such as integrated multi-trophic aquaculture (IMTA) exemplify how ecological principles can align with economic output, creating systems in which different species are farmed together synergistically.

The sustainable management of fisheries is a narrative of both caution and hope. Implementing quotas, seasonal closures, and protected areas helps to balance species preservation with the needs of fishing communities. By employing science-based management, fisheries can remain viable businesses without compromising the marine ecosystems on which they depend.

Marine bioprospecting opens new economic avenues as scientists discover novel compounds in ocean species that can lead to the development of new medicines, biotechnologies, and industrial applications. As we explore these depths, ethical considerations of benefit-sharing and the protection of marine genetic resources are paramount to ensure this frontier benefits all humanity.

Investment in ocean monitoring and governance is also an investment in our economic future. Establishing marine spatial planning and strong regulatory frameworks encourages sustainable practices that shield ecosystems and support economic vitality. The concept of "blue economy" is becoming a pillar in policymaking, promoting the idea that the sustainable use of ocean resources can lead to economic growth while securing the health of the ocean environment.

Education and capacity building are vital economic investments, providing communities with the knowledge and skills needed to engage in sustainable ocean-based economies. Empowered communities can act as stewards, ensuring the oceans' riches are harnessed thoughtfully and with foresight.

It's clear the ocean's economic and ecological narratives are inherently linked; we cannot sustain one without the other. By reconciling the drive for economic development with an imperative for conservation, a new ethos is taking hold, one in which humanity recognizes the need to maintain the health of the oceans as a shared heritage.

As we stand on the shores of possibility, the path forward calls for collaboration between economists, scientists, policymakers, and communities. United in a common purpose, we can align conservation with economic opportunity, demonstrate the viability of sustainable ocean economies, and witness the dawn of an era in which the very safeguarding of our marine commons fuels the prosperity of nations.

The oceans whisper to us of untold riches—not those that can be plundered, but those that, if revered and protected, promise a wealth of sustainable treasures. It is within our grasp to unlock this ocean value, to champion a blue economy that secures livelihoods and sustains ecosystems. Let us, together, unleash the true value of our oceans, ensuring a legacy of bounty and beauty beneath the waves for generations to come.

Regulating Earth: The Oceanic Climate Connection

The vast ocean is a climatic powerhouse, an immense force that regulates temperatures, shapes weather patterns, and sustains life on Earth. It is, without a doubt, one of our greatest allies in the face of climate change. Yet, to harness its full potential in moderating the Earth's climate, we must understand the depth and breadth of this connection and take decisive action to preserve it.

The ocean's role in climate regulation functions through a series of intricate processes. One such process is the oceanic conveyor belt, or thermohaline circulation, which moves warm and cold water around the globe. This circulation acts like a planetary thermostat, not only distributing heat, but also influencing precipitation and wind patterns critical to climate systems.

Perhaps one of the most vital roles the ocean plays in climate regulation is its ability to sequester carbon dioxide (CO_2). Phytoplankton, marine organisms that photosynthesize, draw down CO_2 from the atmosphere and convert it into organic matter that can then sink to the ocean floor. The deep ocean has been a significant carbon sink, absorbing approximately 30% of the human-produced CO_2 since the industrial revolution.

However, this service is not without cost. The absorption of CO_2 leads to ocean acidification, as the gas reacts with seawater to form carbonic acid. This changing chemistry weakens marine shells and skeletons, disrupts physiological processes, and poses a severe threat to marine biodiversity, particularly for shell-forming organisms.

Beyond chemistry, the physical impact of a warming ocean is manifested in the form of rising sea levels, resulting from both melting polar ice caps and thermal expansion as water warms. The consequences for coastal communities worldwide are profound, threatening to redraw maps with the encroachment of the sea.

But the ocean's resilience holds promise for climate mitigation strategies. Marine renewable energies—such as offshore wind, tidal, and wave energy—offer tremendous potential for low-carbon power sources. By capitalizing on these resources, we can reduce our reliance on fossil fuels—a significant contributor to global warming.

Moreover, our understanding of the ocean's carbon cycle has fueled ideas like blue carbon ecosystems—coastal habitats including mangroves, seagrasses, and salt marshes that efficiently store carbon in their biomass and sediments. Protecting these ecosystems can both mitigate climate change and enhance coastal resilience.

To ensure a stable climate, we must also turn to sustainable fisheries management. Overfishing disrupts marine food webs and depletes species that are critical in carbon cycling. A sustainable approach ensures fish populations can rebound and continue to contribute to the ocean's regulatory functions.

Protecting the ocean is a dual-edged sword in climate strategies. We must build resilience by fostering adaptive measures such as constructing sea walls, restoring wetlands, and developing early warning systems for extreme weather events linked to oceanic changes.

While these strategies present a blueprint for action, achieving them requires a global effort. Policies aimed at reducing emissions, coupled with international agreements like the Paris Agreement, are steps in the right direction. However, nations must uphold their commitments and work collaboratively to see tangible results.

Emerging technologies offer renewed hope for ocean–climate intertwinement. Advancements in satellite monitoring and AI can bolster our understanding of ocean dynamics and help predict climate impacts more accurately. This technology could lead to more effective global climate models and, consequently, better mitigation and adaptation measures.

Public engagement is another crucial front. Local communities, often the stewards of their marine environments, can lead conservation efforts with proper support and empowerment. Educating citizens about their connection to the ocean and its role in global climate instills a sense of responsibility and spurs grassroots initiatives.

The ocean–climate connection is fundamental to life on Earth, yet so delicate. As we chart our course toward a sustainable future, we must not overlook the ocean's central role in this journey. It is not only our heritage but our lifeline, and its preservation is inexorably woven into the fabric of our collective action against the existential threat of climate change.

To conclude, while we stand on the precipice of irreversible climatic shifts, the ocean offers us a lifeline. It is a powerful ally that, if respected and protected, can help steady our climate and sustain future generations. The challenge is monumental, but the path is clear: We must integrate the ocean into our climate action plans, marshal resources, and ignite the political will to safeguard this vital organ of our planet. Our successes—

and indeed our very survival—may well depend on the constancy of the rolling sea.

Perils Under the Deep Blue: Marine Challenges

Upon exploring the intrinsic values and myriad benefits our oceans bestow, we can't help but confront the stark challenges facing these vital marine commons. The very fabric of our blue planet's health hinges on the efficacy of addressing the perils that threaten marine ecosystems. Rising sea levels, ocean acidification, temperature shifts, overfishing, plastic pollution, habitat destruction, and bycatch casualties are just a handful of the formidable obstacles plaguing ocean life and stability.

The rising temperatures of our atmosphere don't halt at the ocean's edge; they penetrate the depths, altering marine ecosystems with debilitating effects on species and habitats. One of oceanography's most pressing concerns is how marine life adapts—or fails to adapt—to these shifting temperatures. Warmer waters cause coral bleaching and the death of these ecosystems, resulting in catastrophic impacts on the biodiversity they support.

Acidification presents another insidious side effect of climate change. As seawater absorbs CO_2, its chemistry changes, affecting the ability of creatures like oysters, clams, and corals to build their calcium carbonate shells and skeletons. The implications of this for marine food webs and human industries reliant on these organisms are vast and not fully understood.

Overfishing depletes fish populations faster than they can replenish, destroying the ecological balance of the marine environment. The global fishery crisis is not an abstract concept but a tangible reality in which popular species have been fished to near extinction. This voracious harvest of the ocean not only diminishes fish stocks, but also disrupts the intricate food webs that maintain the ocean's health and functionality.

Plastic pollution is a visually striking and chemically invasive insult to the marine commons. From the largest patches of floating debris to the microscopic particulates ingested by marine organisms, plastics impose a dire threat to marine life and introduce toxins into the food chain. The ubiquity of plastic wastes defines a human mark impervious to the biodegradative processes that keep natural ecosystems in balance.

Habitat destruction—be it from trawling, coastal development, or pollution—erodes biodiversity and strips the ocean of its capacity to house and nurture life. Seagrasses, mangroves, and coral reefs, which play critical roles in carbon sequestration and act as nurseries for a myriad of species, are particularly vulnerable to such destruction.

Bycatch, the incidental capture of non-target species during commercial fishing, often cuts short the lives of countless marine creatures, including species at risk of extinction such as sea turtles, dolphins, and seabirds. This collateral damage in the pursuit of seafood undermines conservation efforts and pushes certain species closer to the brink.

Beyond these biological and chemical threats, the technological and infrastructural inadequacies for marine conservation loom large. The ocean's vastness and depth present logistical nightmares for monitoring, enforcement, and cleanup. It's not merely a matter of scientific understanding but of political will and innovation deployment.

Furthermore, maritime transport, oil extraction, and seabed mining destructively crisscross beneath the waves. These activities mark the oceans with scars that leach chemicals and noise, interrupting the natural order and serene silence of the deep.

The intricate dance between freshwater and saltwater, vital to species that depend on both habitats, is faltering as dams, dikes, and other human-made barriers disrupt natural water flows. Anadromous fish species, those that migrate up rivers from the sea to spawn, face treacherous impediments, threatening their very survival and the ecosystems dependent on them.

Amid all these perils, perhaps the most ubiquitous is the silent spread of "dead zones"—areas so deprived of oxygen that most marine life can't survive. Excessive nutrient pollution from land-based human activities is the primary cause, stimulating algal blooms that, upon decomposition, deplete the oxygen essential for marine life.

As invasive species are inadvertently or intentionally introduced into new marine environments, they wage biological invasions that can unravel local ecosystems. Their uncontrolled spread can decimate native populations and alter habitats, resulting in a loss of native biodiversity and significant economic costs.

The arising socioeconomic repercussions of these perils can't be overstated. Communities relying on fisheries for livelihoods face grave uncertainty as fish stocks dwindle. Coastal regions are at increased risk of storm surges and erosion as protective marine ecosystems degrade. The marine challenges we face are intertwined with human fortunes, emphasizing the urgent need for transformative management and conservation strategies.

To harness the collective will necessary to face these challenges, we must see ourselves as part of the marine ecosystem, not as separate entities that dictate its fate from above. Our fates are as intertwined with the health of the oceans as are the lives of the smallest phytoplankton to the largest whales. The stewardship of our marine commons requires an enlightened appreciation for the intricate connections within this realm—connections we're only beginning to fully understand.

We stand at a precipice where the actions we take—or fail to take—in guarding the marine commons now will echo across generations. It's a call to the caretakers of our blue planet to rise to the challenge with the same depth of determination and innovation shown by the ocean itself. With resolve and ingenuity, we can forge a path that not only steers us away from these perils, but also propels us toward a future in which the ocean continues to thrive, for all its denizens and for ourselves.

Reserves of Hope: The Influence of Marine Protected Areas (MPAs)

In the Earth's biosphere, the ocean provides a subtle yet powerful melody, underpinning the ecological balance and economic vitality of our planet. Yet, like a delicate instrument, it remains vulnerable to misuse and harm. Enter Marine Protected Areas (MPAs)—sanctuaries where the ecological integrity of marine environments is prioritized, showcasing not only the virtue of preservation, but also the potential for restoration and resilience.

The concept behind MPAs isn't novel; rather, it reverberates with our innate understanding of the need for refuge and recovery. We're momentarily stepping back, allowing ecosystems to thrive. MPAs encompass a wide range of marine environments—from coastal estuaries to deep-sea ecosystems—where regulations safeguard biodiversity, ensuring ecosystems can function and species can replenish.

Further, MPAs highlight the nuanced interplay between conservation and human activity. Outcomes vary, but the most effective MPAs share common threads: robust legal frameworks, clear management objectives, adequate enforcement, and the involvement of local communities. This blend of elements cultivates a foundation upon which ecosystems can recuperate and flourish.

Empirical evidence manifests the influence MPAs exert on marine biodiversity. Studies have shown that well-managed MPAs harbor significantly higher numbers of large fish and possess greater species richness than surrounding areas. This increased biomass within MPAs doesn't just linger at the boundaries but spills over, replenishing adjacent fishing grounds and, thus, intertwining conservation with economic gains.

The role of MPAs transcends beyond protecting biodiversity; they serve as benchmark environments. Herein, scientists can discern the undisturbed dynamics of marine life, crafting an understanding that informs broader oceanic resource management. Amidst an era of climate change, MPAs act as control sites, helping us gauge the impacts of human activity on marine ecosystems.

Yet, the establishment of MPAs can be fraught with challenges. Stakeholder conflicts often emerge when immediate economic interests are pitted against long-term environmental stewardship. The path forward necessitates a dialogue that aligns local needs with global environmental imperatives, fostering a sense of stewardship that transcends parochial views.

Community engagement represents a cornerstone of successful MPA policy. When locals are involved—from fishermen to business owners—and the benefits of MPAs become tangible, compliance and active participation in conservation efforts are heightened. This bottom-up approach not only engenders local custodianship, but also facilitates the integration of Indigenous knowledge with scientific insights, forming a potent alliance for marine stewardship.

Furthermore, MPAs contribute to the socioeconomic fabric of their locales. Ecotourism, often entwined with MPAs, demonstrates that intact ecosystems hold incalculable value. It provides economic incentives for conservation while heightening public awareness and appreciation of marine biodiversity. Thus, MPAs extend an invitation for humanity to foster a reverential and sustainable relationship with the oceanic frontier.

In the quest for climate change mitigation, MPAs offer a beacon of hope. Protecting critical habitats such as mangroves, seagrass beds, and coral reefs within MPAs ensures the continuation of natural processes that contribute significantly to carbon sequestration. Recognizing this value is pivotal in the larger narrative of global climate resilience.

Despite their proven benefits, MPAs cover a mere fraction of the world's oceans. The ambition of designating 30% of our oceans as MPAs by 2030, as discussed by international coalitions, isn't an arbitrary target but one rooted in scientific inquiry, aiming to preserve not just isolated pockets of biodiversity but the structural integrity of marine ecosystems at large.

Addressing MPAs' challenges, from legal to enforcement issues, is vital to their success. International collaboration and capacity building can play instrumental roles in overcoming these hurdles. The expansion of MPAs is, therefore, not only an ecological necessity but a test of our collective resolve to steward the marine commons effectively.

Technology serves as an ally in this endeavor, enabling enhanced monitoring and management of MPAs. Remote sensing, autonomous vehicles, and advances in data analysis provide the means to observe and act upon the dynamics within protected zones, ensuring the pulses of recovery and regeneration are felt and fostered.

MPAs, by their very nature, are long-term engagements. The protective benefits they offer often materialize over timeframes that may surpass immediate economic cycles and political tenures. This necessitates a vision that respects the slow, yet profound, pace of ecological processes—a testament to the intrinsic value and innate resilience of marine life.

Within our hands lies the opportunity to amplify the influence of MPAs—an avenue to not only stem the tide of marine degradation but to actively rehabilitate our oceanic commons. It's a chance to reaffirm our kinship with the sea and to reignite a collective ambition for a future in which marine life thrives alongside human endeavors.

As we chart the course of our environmental legacy, let the reserves of hope embodied by MPAs kindle the realization that the fate of the oceans is undeniably intertwined with our own. It's a call to preserve the sanctity of the marine commons—for the oceans do not belong to us, we belong to them. Their well-being is an irrevocable part of our survival and prosperity.

Steering the Course: Innovations in Ocean Guardianship

The guardianship of our oceans is an endeavor that resonates with the essence of our existence on this blue planet. As we explore the myriad ways in which we can protect these vast expanses, innovation emerges as a beacon of hope. Technology and ingenuity are casting new light on paths to marine conservation, offering us the tools to not only understand, but also effectively guard our marine commons.

Ocean monitoring technologies have evolved exponentially, propelling our knowledge forward. Satellite surveillance systems enable us to keep vigilant watch over the seas, detecting illegal fishing activities with precision. Better monitoring heralds a new era in which sustainable fishing practices aren't just encouraged but enforced, safeguarding our marine ecosystems against overexploitation.

Advancements in autonomous vehicles, such as underwater drones equipped with sensors and cameras, are giving us new perspectives of the ocean's depths. These robotic explorers traverse areas once inaccessible to humans, mapping the seafloor and studying marine life to collect essential data for effective ocean management.

The concept of marine protected areas (MPAs) has been revolutionized by technology. Electronic tracking and geofencing technologies ensure MPAs are more than lines on a map; they enable real-time management and prevent incursions, providing sanctuaries for marine life to flourish away from human pressures.

Climate change poses an existential threat to our oceans, prompting the quest for innovative carbon sequestration methods. Research into the cultivation of kelp forests and seagrass meadows offers a natural way to absorb carbon dioxide, while also providing habitat for marine species. These blue carbon initiatives represent a harmonious marriage of nature conservation and climate mitigation strategies.

The field of genomics has found its way into ocean stewardship. By sequencing the DNA of marine organisms, conservationists can monitor biodiversity at a granular level, revealing the health of marine populations and facilitating the restoration of endangered species. Genetic insights also arm us against the silent threat of invasive species, offering methods to detect and manage them before ecological havoc ensues.

A truly groundbreaking innovation is the incorporation of artificial intelligence (AI) into ocean research. AI algorithms analyze vast amounts of data collected from the marine environment, identifying patterns and changes that would take humans years to uncover. This ability to swiftly process information accelerates our response to conservation challenges.

The power of citizen science has also been amplified through the digital revolution. Mobile apps and online platforms enable countless individuals around the globe to contribute to data collection and ocean watch efforts. Each submission adds to a collective database, which leads to a more inclusive and comprehensive framework for ocean stewardship.

The scourge of plastic pollution has spurred inventors and environmentalists to devise novel cleanup solutions. Projects like The Ocean Cleanup have come to symbolize proactive action as they aim to filter out debris from the world's waters using advanced technologies while minimizing impact on marine life.

Corporate responsibility is increasingly important in the sphere of ocean guardianship. Companies harnessing the power of the blue economy are adopting "net positive" approaches, innovating in sectors like shipping and fisheries to reduce their ecological footprints. This initiative values the health of the ocean as intrinsic to long-term business success, aligning industry with ecology.

Aquaculture, too, is undergoing a transformation. Innovations are optimizing sustainable fish farming, minimizing the release of pollutants, and implementing recirculating systems that conserve water and energy, crafting a more harmonious relationship with our oceanic resources.

As we look to the horizon, advances in marine renewable energy promise a twofold benefit—reducing our carbon footprint while harnessing the boundless kinetic energy of the seas. Wave and tidal energy projects are being designed to operate symbiotically with marine ecosystems, providing clean power while protecting oceanic life.

Education and collaboration are also key ingredients in steering the course of ocean guardianship. Innovative outreach programs are cultivating a new generation of ocean stewards—equipped with knowledge and passion for marine conservation, they're poised to be the voices and hands preserving our marine commons.

Innovation in ocean guardianship is a tapestry woven with threads of science, technology, and human resolve. It encapsulates our pursuit to defend the oceans not as distant stewards but as intimate allies. Our efforts to forge new tools and methods stand as testaments to our responsibility and our capacity for stewardship of our planet's most defining feature—the ocean.

For we are at a pivotal juncture in our relationship with the seas that cradle life as we know it. With each stride in technology and every innovative approach, we are learning to better read the rhythms of the tides, the calls of the deep, and the needs of the marine symphony. Instead of silencing this orchestra of life as our past actions have, we are now striving to compose a new future—one of balance, harmony, and shared guardianship.

Chapter 7:
Waste Not:
The Circular Economy's March Forward

Within the spiraling narrative of human progress, the concept of waste as a dismissible byproduct is being boldly reimagined through the transformative lens of the circular economy. In "Waste Not: The Circular Economy's March Forward," we embark on a paradigm shift that rejects the traditional linear economy's "take-make-dispose" approach, favoring instead a regenerative system that designs out waste, keeps products in use, and maintains materials within closed-loop cycles.

This chapter illuminates the trail of innovation that is rerouting the trajectory of our consumptive practices toward a more sustainable and resilient future. Through modern alchemy, waste materials continuously flow into new forms, reducing the need for virgin resources and diminishing the burden on our planet's finite reserves.

As we delve into the circular economy, we explore not just the commendable environmental outcomes, but also the enhanced economic stability and social cohesion that emerge from this restorative model. The ethos of resource efficiency and value retention weaves through the narratives of industries and individuals alike, compelling us to redefine growth, empower communities, and free ourselves from the shackles of wastefulness. The march forward is marked by a spirit of adaptive ingenuity, a testament to humanity's capacity for renewal and relentless drive toward a balanced coexistence with Earth's ecosystems.

Circular Economy: Concept and Benefits

In our relentless pursuit of a sustainable future, the concept of a circular economy has emerged as a beacon of hope, illuminating the path away from our traditional "take-make-dispose" model. At its core, the circular economy seeks to redefine growth, focusing on societal benefits as a whole. It's underpinned by a transition to renewable energy sources, waste reduction, and an inclusive approach to economic health that aims to decouple growth from resource consumption.

The circular economy is predicated on three fundamental principles: design out waste and pollution, keep products and materials in use, and regenerate natural systems. By adopting this model, businesses can create opportunities for growth that are not contingent upon the exploitation of finite resources.

There are profound benefits to this transition, not least of which is the mitigation of environmental impact. In a circular system, waste is not merely "managed" but eliminated through superior design and maintenance practices. This fosters a closed-loop system in which materials are persistently recycled, remanufactured, or repurposed.

But the circular economy isn't just about environmental stewardship—it's also economically smart. By embracing reuse, companies can shield themselves from volatility in resource prices. This generates economic stability and offers a competitive edge. Furthermore, circular business models encourage innovation, drive job creation in the recycling and servicing sectors, and promote local development.

Another significant benefit is the reduction of carbon emissions. By prioritizing regenerative resources and remanufacturing processes, the circular economy decreases the demand for energy-intensive production, thus, lowering the carbon footprint of goods and services. This is vital in our struggle against climate change and crucial in achieving targets set by international accords.

Moreover, a circular economy promotes resource efficiency. It encourages extending the life cycle of products through repair, refurbishment, and remanufacturing, which reduces the need to extract new resources. This not only conserves raw materials, but also minimizes the degradative effect on biodiversity and ecosystems.

From a social perspective, the circular economy opens a realm of opportunities for consumer engagement. The shift toward service-based models changes the notion of ownership, leading to products-as-a-service arrangements. This can democratize access to various goods, as products become services and experiences, opening new avenues for societal inclusivity.

The circular economy holds particular promise for developing regions, where resource constraints are often more pronounced. It can catalyze local economic activity and empower communities by localizing production and closing the loop on material flows, fostering resilience against global market disruptions.

However, seizing these opportunities is not without its challenges. Transitioning to a circular economy requires a paradigm shift in mindset, design, and practice. It necessitates broad-based collaboration among manufacturers, consumers, lawmakers, and waste management entities to create closed-loop systems in which resources circulate with minimal loss.

Policies play a key role in fostering the transition. Governments can incentivize circular business models through tax reforms, subsidies, and regulations. For instance, extended producer responsibility regulations can prompt companies to consider the end-of-life stage of their products, effectively internalizing the cost of waste.

Education is another pillar. Consumers and manufacturers alike need to be informed about the merits and strategies of circular economies to inspire participation. Educational initiatives can dispel misconceptions, spotlight best practices, and inspire innovation driven by circular economy principles.

What's striking about the circular economy is its intrinsic link to innovation; not only in the development of new materials and production processes, but also in fostering generative business models that disrupt industries. This could pave the way for a more sustainable global economy that is robust, efficient, and capable of meeting our present and future needs.

In summary, the benefits of a circular economy are manifold, ranging from environmental restoration and economic resilience to social inclusion and innovation. While the road to a wholly circular economy is undeniably complex and challenging, its potential to reshape our world for the better is boundlessly rewarding. Adapting to its tenets can help us steer our planet toward a sustainable future that cherishes and preserves resources for generations to come.

As we look ahead and gear up for the sustainable revolutions of the twenty-first century, the circular economy stands as a pivotal element in our collective quest. It is not just an alternative to our prevailing linear economy; it is an undeniable imperative as we tread toward a future where we "waste not" and tread gently upon this Earth we call home.

Global Waste Saga: Challenges and Transformations

The journey toward a circular economy is riddled with roadblocks and challenges, but it is also marked by remarkable transformations. The global waste saga has been a complex tale of unbridled consumption and its consequent debris that has plagued our planet. With the rising tide of waste reaching every corner of the world, the need for sustainable waste management practices becomes more pressing every day. The urgency is underscored by the stark reality that only a fraction of waste is currently managed sustainably.

Historically, waste was either incinerated, buried, or left in open dumps. However, each of these methods carries detrimental consequences for both the environment and human health. Incineration releases toxic pollutants into the air, landfills leach harmful chemicals into the soil and groundwater, and open dumps serve as breeding grounds for disease-carrying pests. These archaic practices underscore the depth of our challenge as we seek to overhaul systems that have long been ingrained in our society.

One glaring issue within our global waste conundrum is the proliferation of single-use plastics. These convenient, yet environmentally devastating materials find their way into our oceans and landscapes, contributing to the destruction of ecosystems. Approximately 8 million tons of plastic are dumped into the ocean each year, evidencing a crisis that demands immediate action and innovative solutions.

Another challenge is electronic waste, or e-waste, which embodies a rapidly growing stream of discarded items. The toxins and valuable resources contained within such waste can cause environmental harm if improperly managed, and yet they also represent a substantial opportunity for recovery and reuse. The pattern of short-lived electronics exacerbates the problem, creating a waste cycle that our current systems are ill-equipped to handle.

Addressing these complexities in waste management requires systematic changes and the adoption of the circular economy model, which stands in stark contrast to the currently dominant linear economy. The linear "take-make-dispose" model appears ever more inadequate in a world striving for sustainability. The shift toward circularity focuses on designing out waste, keeping products and materials in use, and regenerating natural systems.

One transformative approach becoming increasingly popular is the concept of "Zero Waste." Zero Waste strategies aim to redesign the life cycle of products so all resources are reused and nothing is sent to landfills or incinerators. Such strategies require significant shifts in product design, consumer behavior, and corporate responsibility.

The automotive and technology sectors are among those leading the way in incorporating circular principles. For instance, car manufacturers are exploring ways to ensure vehicles are not only recyclable but actually composed of recycled materials. Similarly, tech companies are finding innovative methods to reduce e-waste through modular design, facilitating repair and component upgrades rather than whole-unit disposal.

In the realm of plastics, innovative materials are being developed to combat the single-use plastic crisis. Bioplastics, which are made from renewable biomaterials, promise a reduced environmental footprint. We must be wary of their own complexities regarding end-of-life management and potential competition with food resources, though.

At the municipal level, integrated waste management systems are being adopted in progressive cities worldwide. These systems focus on waste segregation, controlled disposal, recycling, and energy recovery, but they require significant investment and public cooperation. Cities that excel in waste management are often characterized by high public awareness and strong policy support.

In developing nations, the formalization of waste picker communities plays a vital role in managing recyclables. These communities divert substantial amounts of waste from landfills, yet they often work in deplorable conditions. By integrating these informal sectors into the official waste management plan, we can improve both their livelihoods and the overall efficiency of waste management.

On the legislative front, extended producer responsibility (EPR) laws compel companies to be accountable for the end of life of their products, providing economic incentives to design more sustainable goods. EPR represents a policy evolution in which the responsibility is shared across the product life cycle rather than burdening consumers or municipalities alone with waste disposal.

Technological innovation also emerges as a cornerstone of the evolution of waste management. Advancements in material science, waste sorting, and recycling technologies hold the potential to recover more materials with greater efficiency. Innovations such as chemical recycling of plastics could revolutionize the recycling industry by breaking down plastics into their monomers for repurposing.

Despite these advancements, the push toward a truly circular economy in which all waste is repurposed faces numerous challenges, the biggest being the entrenchment of old habits and economic models. Transitioning requires not only new systems and technologies, but also changes in cultural attitudes and values. The complexity of modern products and globalization further complicates the transition, requiring international cooperation and standards.

However, there is hope. Each successful example of circular waste management illuminates the path forward for others to follow. The waste saga we are part of is evolving from a tale of woe to one of opportunity. As we continue this journey, the transformations we make hold the promise of a more sustainable future.

By reimagining our relationship with waste and striving for a circular economy, we are not just solving a logistical challenge; we are redefining our cultural ethos toward stewardship and sustainability. Such profound transformation has the power to mitigate the pressing environmental crises of our time, while fostering economic and social resilience.

Embracing these changes and pushing the boundaries of innovation, we can rewrite the global waste saga into a narrative of regeneration and renewal, pivotal to the advancement of the circular economy's march forward.

Toward Sustainable Waste Management: Future Directions

The journey to a sustainable future is paved with innovation, dedication, and tireless pursuit of new methodologies in waste management. Embracing the principles of the circular economy, we seek not only to reduce the burdens our consumption inflicts upon the Earth but to envision waste as a resource, opening pathways for recovery and rebirth.

This section endeavors to illuminate the optimistic trajectories in which waste is not an endpoint but a new beginning.

The circular economy compels us to redefine our relationship with materials and resources. Its crescendo lies in eliminating "waste" from our vocabulary by employing an ecologically aligned design that integrates end-of-life planning at the inception of products and processes. With global populations predicted to swell and urban density intensifying, future-forward waste management solutions call for a blended approach of policy reform, technological innovation, and societal participation.

At the policy level, regulations and incentives are paramount. Governments around the world must galvanize transition by drafting legislation that incentivizes circular practices. Tax breaks, subsidies, and grants can motivate businesses to adopt circular principles. Additionally, regulatory frameworks such as extended producer responsibility (EPR) need to become standard practice, compelling manufacturers to bear the cost of disposal and recycling, thus, encouraging them to design for longevity and recyclability.

When it comes to technology, the horizon gleams with potential. Advancements in sorting and recycling technologies afford greater precision and recovery rates. Biotechnology offers promising ventures into bio-based materials and energy generation from organic waste. Moreover, digitization, including the Internet of Things (IoT), could usher in unparalleled efficiency in waste collection and processing, minimizing leakage into the environment.

The societal aspect of waste management cannot be overstated. Education and community engagement play a crucial role in bringing circular economy principles to life. Programs that enlighten citizens about the value of reducing, reusing, and recycling create a culture of mindfulness around consumption and waste. Initiatives like repair cafés and tool libraries can help foster a sense of ownership and responsibility toward shared community resources.

Corporate dynamics are also shifting. Companies increasingly understand that sustainable waste practices can lead to cost savings, enhanced brand reputation, and novel revenue streams. The business case for circularity is being made and remade across diverse industries. Business models such as product-as-a-service, in which value is maintained through leasing products rather than outright sale, also contribute to the reduction of waste and extend product life cycles.

At the intersection of policy, technology, business, and societal change lies the realm of innovation. For waste management to be truly sustainable, continuous innovation in material science is essential. Materials of the future must be not just recyclable, but also biodegradable and non-toxic, returning to the Earth without causing harm. The development of such materials represents a grand challenge that, if met, could fundamentally alter the trajectory of waste management.

Another significant development on the horizon is advancements in waste-to-energy technologies. By converting waste streams into usable energy, such systems not only provide a sustainable energy source, but also mitigate the volume of waste destined for landfill sites. As renewable energy becomes more pervasive, waste-to-energy solutions could play a substantial role in both energy generation and waste reduction.

Standardization and interoperability of products and components promote an ease of recycling and reuse that is not currently present. Imagine a world where, for example, electronic devices are designed with common standards, enabling easier and more complete recycling. Such a paradigm shift requires industry-wide collaboration and a commitment to unified sustainability guidelines.

Urban planning has a substantial influence on waste management prospects. Smart cities, built with sustainability as a foundation, utilize intelligent systems to reduce waste generation and optimize resource use. The planning of such cities must involve waste minimization considerations, including the placement and operation of recycling and composting facilities within easy reach.

While looking forward, it's also imperative to borrow wisdom from traditional and Indigenous practices. Many Indigenous cultures have utilized circular principles harmoniously with nature for millennia. Modern systems can synergize this ancestral knowledge with current scientific understanding to achieve more holistic and effective waste management solutions.

Looking even further ahead, it is clear global collaboration is required to implement sustainable waste management practices effectively. Shared strategies and technologies can be tailored to fit the unique needs and capabilities of different regions. Moreover, collaboration can facilitate the transfer of knowledge and resources to developing regions, where waste management infrastructure may be less established.

Finally, within this future mosaic of waste management, resilience should be a critical feature. Systems must be designed to not just cope with but thrive amid changes, whether they be climatic, economic, or social. A robust framework of waste management is one that is adaptable and prepared for unexpected challenges, ensuring its longevity for generations to come.

The path toward sustainable waste management is unpaved and sometimes beset with obstacles, yet it is ripe with potential. It is a path we must not only travel, but also construct as we go, laying down the stones of innovation, policy, collaboration, and education for a more sustainable tomorrow. Our march forward is not just an imperative, it is an opportunity to re-envision our world into one where every product, every material, and every person has a meaningful place in the circle of reuse and regeneration.

Chapter 8:
Biodiversity's Beacon:
Safeguarding Our Natural Heritage

As we delve into the essence of biodiversity, envision it not as a mere collection of flora and fauna, but as a symphony of life in which every organism plays a critical role in maintaining ecological harmony. The previous chapter guided us through the virtues of the circular economy, a harbinger of sustainable resource management. Building on that foundation, "Biodiversity's Beacon: Safeguarding Our Natural Heritage" casts a light on the intrinsic value of Earth's rich tapestry of life.

Here, we explore the gravity of biodiversity loss and assess its implications through a multifaceted lens, encompassing both ecological and human-centric views. We'll unite under the cause for preserving what David Attenborough calls "our greatest treasure" and confront the challenges—ensuring the endurance of our natural heritage.

Strategies for species protection and policies for preservation are meticulously scrutinized, underscoring the imperative for biodiversity integrity. Embracing conservation efforts is not only a testament to our respect for the natural world, but a necessity for the well-being of our own species. As stewards of Earth, it is our duty to shield this beacon of biodiversity, not only as an ethical mandate but as a vital step toward a sustainable future for all inhabitants of our planet.

Unraveling Biodiversity: Life's Network

"Biodiversity" is not merely a catalogue of species; it embodies the intricate network of life in which each thread is a lifeline, connecting organisms to each other and to their environment. As guardians of our natural heritage, it is essential to comprehend the fabric of life and to appreciate the richness of biodiversity that sustains our planet.

In the magnificence of a rainforest or the splendor of a coral reef lies a symphony of ecological interactions. These ecosystems, powered by an array of species, form a complex web of life that is much more than the sum of its parts. Each life form—from the microscopic mycorrhizal fungi nurturing the soil, to the majestic elephants shaping the African savanna—has a part to play. Together, they orchestrate the processes that make Earth habitable for us all.

The concept of biodiversity extends beyond the presence of diverse life forms and includes genetic diversity, species diversity, and ecological diversity. This triad ensures adaptability and resilience in the face of environmental change. It is this diversity that buffers ecosystems against shocks and stresses, allowing them to recover from disturbances like wildfires, storms, and disease outbreaks.

However, just as every craftsman knows, the strength of a fabric lies in the interweaving of its threads. The same is true for biodiversity. Interactions among species—such as pollination, seed dispersal, and predator-prey dynamics—are critical to the flow of energy and nutrients through an ecosystem. With each extinction, we lose not only a species, but also its unique role and the benefits it provided within its ecological network.

Modern science has begun to unravel the complexity of these interactions. Research shows more diverse ecosystems are more productive and resilient. This isn't just about numbers; it's about the connections and the quality of relationships within the biological community. In evolutionary terms, these relationships have been refined over countless generations, leading to highly optimized systems.

Understanding these relationships is not just about scientific curiosity; there are real-world implications for humanity. The interconnectedness of life's network supports many services on which we rely—services such as pollination of crops, regulation of climate, water purification, and disease control. These ecosystem services are the foundation upon which we build our economies, secure our food, and nurture our health.

The loss of biodiversity means the unraveling of these services and, ultimately, the undermining of human well-being. It is not an overstatement to claim that as biodiversity diminishes, so does the quality of human life. This relationship is especially poignant for Indigenous communities and rural populations that directly depend on the health of their surrounding ecosystems for survival.

It's worth noting that biodiversity hotspots, areas with exceptionally high levels of endemic species, are experiencing particularly intense pressure from human activities. The conservation of these hotspots isn't just about preserving the scenic beauty or charismatic fauna; it's about ensuring the persistence of crucial genetic resources that may hold the keys to future medical advances or agricultural improvements.

Human activities have reshaped the landscape of our planet, and as a result, we are witnessing an era of mass extinctions. Habitat loss, climate change, pollution, overexploitation, and invasive species are the harbingers of this biodiversity crisis. They act synergistically to erode the intricate tapestry of life at an alarming rate. Recognizing these threats is the first step toward mitigating them.

The urgency to protect and restore biodiversity is unarguably linked to the need for sustainable development. Economies should be molded around the conservation of ecosystems rather than the exploitation of them. Sustainable practices are not just an alternative but an imperative for survivability—for both non-human species and ourselves.

If we are to safeguard biodiversity, we must integrate its value into our societal and economic structures. This involves embracing a conservation ethic that recognizes the intrinsic value of all life forms, as well as their utilitarian value to humanity. A multi-pronged strategy that combines conservation efforts within protected areas with ecological restoration and sustainable use of natural resources is required.

Conserving biodiversity is akin to maintaining the engines and life-support systems of our planet. It is an outright necessity. In this bewilderingly beautiful and complex world, every loss diminishes life's richness, and every conservation victory is a step toward a sustainable future.

As we unfold the biodiversity narrative, it's important to instill a sense of wonder and responsibility toward nature. To lose biodiversity is to silence nature's chorus, leaving us impoverished in more ways than one. Only by valuing life's network in all its forms and functions can we hope to preserve the mosaic of life that sustains us.

The tapestry of life is frayed at the edges, but it is within our hands to weave it back together to reinforce the threads that bind us to nature and to each other. Let us commit to this task with the understanding that our fates are intertwined and that it is in our collective interest to nurture the planet that nourishes us.

In conclusion, as we ponder upon our role within this vast network of life, it becomes undeniably clear that each action we take leaves an imprint. We must choose to be the stewards of biodiversity, the architects of a future that honors and preserves the myriad forms of life upon which we so profoundly depend.

The Vanishing Variance: Assessing Biodiversity Loss

As we delve into the whispering realms of life's rich tapestry, where every filament interweaves with boundless complexity, we stand to behold a lamentable unraveling. Biodiversity, the variance that gives vibrancy and resilience to our natural heritage, is vanishing at an alarming rate. This section unfurls the grave narrative of biodiversity loss, an urgent call to action for all humanity concerned with sustaining the planet's life-support systems.

The term "biodiversity" encompasses the diversity within species, among species, and of ecosystems. It is a crucial element of Earth's survival mechanism, enabling ecosystems to recover from perturbations and providing the raw materials for adaptation and evolutionary processes. Yet, as we incessantly encroach upon natural habitats and overexploit wildlife, the consequence is a stark diminution of biodiversity.

Current assessments reveal Earth is undergoing the sixth mass extinction, with species disappearing at rates hundreds or thousands of times faster than the natural background rate. This rapid erosion of biodiversity implies dire repercussions for ecosystem services upon which human civilization heavily relies, including pollination, nutrient cycling, and climate regulation. The impoverishment of biodiversity also strips away the very essence of many cultural identities and traditional knowledge systems, irrevocably changing the human experience.

The drivers behind such extensive biodiversity loss are multifaceted. The primary culprits include habitat loss due to deforestation, agricultural expansion, and urban development. Overexploitation of species through hunting, fishing, and trade, as well as the pervasive issue of pollution, contribute significantly to the dilemma. Furthermore, invasive species disturb the equilibrium of native ecosystems, and climate change accelerates the rate at which species are unable to adapt, further threatening their survival.

Quantifying biodiversity loss necessitates meticulous scientific inquiry and the synthesis of data from conservation studies, wildlife monitoring, and environmental assessments. The Living Planet Index, which measures the state of the world's biological diversity, indicates there has been a 68% decrease in the size of populations of mammals, birds, fish, reptiles, and amphibians globally between 1970 and 2016. This stark statistic compels the global community to acknowledge that the loss of biodiversity is not only an environmental challenge, but also a development, economic, security, and moral issue.

Marine ecosystems are not immune to this trend. Overfishing, habitat destruction, and climate change imperil the richness of life within our oceans. Coral reefs, the rainforests of the sea, are undergoing extensive bleaching events, with over 50% at risk of disappearing within the next few decades if current trends continue. This loss reverberates through the marine food web and endangers the livelihoods of millions reliant on oceanic resources.

In the realm of flora, the vanishing variance is equally distressing. Plant species are going extinct up to 500 times faster than their natural rates of extinction due to human activity. Their disappearance leads to cascading effects in ecosystems, including the breakdown of plant-pollinator networks and destabilization of soil structures, threatening both wild and agricultural landscapes.

Inland waters, the nerve centers of continental biodiversity, are facing their own crisis. Freshwater habitats are home to more than 10% of all known animal species, many of which are adapted to highly specific ecological niches. However, development pressures, pollution, and the redirection and damming of waterways are causing these species to vanish before they are even discovered.

Even as we grapple with these sobering truths, the means to measure the full extent of biodiversity loss remain imperfect for the simple reason that a vast number of species remain unknown to science. We have documented only about 1.7 million species, with millions more presumed to inhabit especially rich environments such as tropical rainforests and deep-sea ecosystems.

To illuminate the path forward and reverse the trends of biodiversity loss, we must strengthen and integrate conservation efforts with sustainable development principles. Implementing protections such as creating and maintaining protected areas, enforcing wildlife trafficking laws, and engaging in restoration ecology are immediate steps to mitigate the crisis. Moreover, fostering a profound societal shift toward recognizing the intrinsic value of nature is paramount to long-term sustainability.

The conservation community increasingly advocates for the use of nature-based solutions to both mitigate biodiversity loss and adapt to climate change. This nexus approach harnesses ecosystem services to address societal challenges and simultaneously bolster biodiversity. By deploying natural solutions such as reforestation, wetland restoration, and urban green spaces, we can create a win-win situation for our environment and our people.

At the heart of our efforts must be the adoption of transformative changes in our global economic, social, and financial systems. Sustainable production and consumption patterns need to be mainstreamed. Integrating biodiversity values into decision-making processes at all levels is fundamental for making considerable strides.

Amidst these challenges, the role of citizen scientists and Indigenous communities has been recognized as crucial. Their local knowledge and long-term ecological observations are invaluable resources for understanding biodiversity dynamics. Backed by their insights, we can advance conservation science and foster a ground-up approach that complements the top-down strategies of international environmental governance.

In confronting the vanishing variance, we stand before a precipice. Not only does biodiversity loss undermine the resilience of ecosystems and impoverish our world's wondrous variety, it also threatens the very mechanisms that support life on Earth. As we endeavor to preserve what remains and restore what has been lost, embracing sustainability transitions becomes an imperative of our time. It's within our collective capacity to be stewards whose legacy won't be the silence of extinction, but the chorus of revival and renewal.

Through a Human Lens: The Impact on Biodiversity

Biodiversity is the enchanting, rhythmic dance of life on Earth, weaving complex patterns of interdependence and resilience. But this dance is under threat, not from a natural disaster or a celestial event, but from humanity's own actions. As we delve deeper into understanding this rich tapestry, we realize the profound effects our species has had on the planet's biological diversity. The causes are manifold—habitat loss, pollution, climate change, and overexploitation of resources to name a few—and the impacts are far-reaching.

Every time a forest is cleared, we don't just lose trees. We lose the intricate network of life that those trees support. With every acre of rainforest lost, we undercut the stability of global climate patterns and lead countless species toward the brink of extinction. The extensive destruction of habitat fragments populations, leaving them too decimated to recover. This is not just an ecological crisis but an ethical one as well.

The concept of "keystone species" illustrates this perfectly. These species hold an ecosystem together, much like a linchpin. Without them, the ecological structure crumbles, causing cascading effects throughout the food chain. When we disrupt these key species through direct or indirect human actions, we endanger the whole system.

Pollution inflicts its own array of biodiversity consequences. Pesticides, heavy metals, and industrial runoff amass in ecosystems, often leading to eutrophication and the devastation of aquatic life zones. Alarmingly, toxins entering the base of the food web escalate through biomagnification, putting apex predators and, eventually, humans at risk.

Climate change, driven largely by human-induced greenhouse gas emissions, adds another layer of stress. The alteration of global temperature and precipitation patterns pushes species out of their native habitats, resulting in loss of biodiversity and ecosystem services. Corals, for instance, are bleaching at unprecedented rates, jeopardizing marine biodiversity and the livelihoods dependent on healthy ocean ecosystems.

Overexploitation compounds these issues. The unsustainable harvest of plants and animals, whether for traditional medicine, pets, or luxury items, dwindles populations and affects their genetic diversity. Removing individual species in large numbers can disrupt ecological processes, leading to unforeseen consequences, including the loss of potential medicinal resources.

But the human impact is not uniformly negative. There are conservation success stories in which targeted efforts have brought species back from the edge of extinction. The American Bison is a symbol of such an achievement. Once numbering in the tens of millions, the species faced near-extinction in the nineteenth century but have since been revived through dedicated conservation efforts.

Indeed, human-induced biodiversity loss doesn't have to be our legacy. It's within our capacity, and increasingly within our collective will, to mitigate these negative impacts. Recognizing the intrinsic value of biodiversity, societies around the globe are beginning to prioritize sustainable practices and conservation efforts.

Ecotourism serves as a significant example of how human activity can support biodiversity while benefiting local communities. By placing an economic value on intact ecosystems and the species within them, it promotes both biodiversity conservation and local economic development.

The importance of Indigenous and local knowledge in biodiversity conservation can't be overstated either. These communities have lived in harmony with their environment for generations, and their practices often embody sustainable living. Integrating this knowledge with contemporary conservation efforts is key to preserving biodiversity.

Engaging citizens in biodiversity initiatives has also shown to increase awareness and support for conservation efforts. Citizen science projects, for example, empower individuals to contribute to scientific knowledge while fostering a connection with nature. Such involvement can shift public perception and drive policy changes.

Education plays a pivotal role in shaping the human impact on biodiversity. By building curricula around the importance of biodiversity, future generations are armed with the knowledge to make sustainable choices and advocate for policies that protect our natural heritage.

To truly appreciate the human impact on biodiversity, one must consider the value of ecosystems not just in terms of the services they provide us, but also for their intrinsic worth. Each species extinguished is a loss of a unique life form, an irreplaceable piece of the grand evolutionary puzzle.

As stewards of this planet, we are bestowed with not only the power to shape the future of biodiversity, but also the responsibility to safeguard it for generations to come. It is a weighty mantle to carry, but one filled with the opportunity to write a story of reconciliation and restoration.

The connection between human well-being and biodiversity is clear. A diverse, healthy environment contributes to food security, disease regulation, and quality of life. By investing in biodiversity, we invest in ourselves—securing a self-sustaining legacy that honors the interconnected web of life on which we all depend.

In conclusion, through a human lens, the impact on biodiversity can seem daunting. But this perspective also reveals our incredible ability to generate positive change. With informed, passionate, and concerted efforts, we can redirect the course of our environmental narrative from one of destruction to one of preservation and reverence for the rich diversity of life that blooms around us. It is up to us to ensure the symphony of life plays on, and it begins with recognizing and reshaping our impact on the natural world.

In Defense of Diversity: Species Protection

As we navigate the myriad challenges facing our planet, the preservation of biodiversity stands as a formidable bastion against ecological collapse. The necessity of maintaining diverse habitats and ecosystems cannot be overstated, for it is within this diversity that the resilience and stability of our natural world lie. In this context, discussing endangered species becomes a crucial aspect of our stewardship of Earth. Endangered species serve as the proverbial "canaries in the coal mine," indicating the health of our ecosystems and the pressures they face.

Protecting endangered species entails protecting the habitats and ecosystems that sustain them. This is not merely a gesture of goodwill toward the natural world but a fundamental requirement for preserving biodiversity on which human survival ultimately depends. Habitats are not simply environments; they are the complex networks of life that provide services essential to our existence—services such as pollination, water purification, and climate regulation.

The interdependence of species within ecosystems is a tapestry of complex interactions, each organism playing a role that maintains the ecological balance. When one species faces the brink of extinction, it is often a symptom of broader ecosystem degradation. The loss of a single species can have significant cascading effects, as each species often relies on interactions and relationships with others to survive.

An example of the profound impact the loss of a single species can have on an ecosystem is the case of the gray wolf in Yellowstone National Park. Their reintroduction has led to a trophic cascade effect, in which the renewed predation pressure on elk populations has allowed overgrazed habitats to recover, benefiting many other species and leading to greater biodiversity within the park.

The fate of endangered species often mirrors the environmental pressures we ourselves face. Climate change, habitat loss, pollution, and overexploitation are common threats to both the variety of life on Earth and the quality of life for humanity. It is therefore in our best interest to actively protect threatened species and, by extension, the ecosystems they inhabit. The existence of robust species protection policies is not only a moral imperative but a practical strategy for environmental and human well-being.

Species protection is a complex and multifaceted issue, but at its core, it requires establishing and effectively managing protected areas, enforcing anti-poaching laws, regulating and monitoring wildlife trade, and restoring degraded habitats. It's about understanding that each species plays a unique role in its ecosystem, and the extinction of a species can mean the unraveling of ecological processes that have taken millennia to establish.

Furthermore, species protection is deeply intertwined with cultural and economic contexts. Often, the loss of species results in the loss of natural resources that local communities depend on, which can lead to economic hardship and cultural erosion. Conversely, species conservation can provide economic opportunities through ecotourism and sustainable use of natural resources.

For instance, the protection of sea turtle nesting sites not only conserves these ancient mariners, but also encourages ecotourism, providing income for local communities that might otherwise turn to harvesting turtles and their eggs for a living. Such holistic approaches have the potential to create win-win scenarios for biodiversity and human communities.

The complexities involved in species protection necessitate interdisciplinary approaches that combine biological sciences with social sciences, economics, and policy studies. It's an undertaking that requires global cooperation and commitment, as many species cross national boundaries. Policies must be informed by the best available science and be adaptive to change, given the dynamic nature of ecosystems and the threats they face.

Conservation biology, as a discipline, has provided invaluable insights into the methods and strategies for species protection. It underscores the critical importance of genetic diversity within populations, suggesting our approaches to conservation must also ensure the variability that allows species to adapt to changing conditions and, thus, survive in the long run.

As we stand at a crossroads in our relationship with the natural world, embracing the responsibility of species protection is essential. It is a task that requires courage, commitment, and creativity. The protection of endangered species is not just an act of charity toward nature; it is a crucial investment in our continued prosperity and a testament to our capacity for empathy and foresight.

Ultimately, protecting endangered species is about honoring the interconnectedness of life and recognizing every living thing has its place and purpose within the vast mosaic of biodiversity. It's about accepting we are part of a larger whole and the actions we take today will resonate through generations. The task before us is monumental, but so, too, is the opportunity to redefine our legacy as a species that not only survives but thrives in harmony with the natural world.

To this end, species protection is not simply another item on a list of environmental tasks; it is, rather, an embodiment of the respect and adoration we hold for life in its myriad forms. It signifies a commitment to not just endure but to enrich the world we live in, ensuring a future in which nature's chorus sings as richly and diversely as it has since time immemorial.

Conserving the Web of Life: Policies for Preservation

In the shadow of our ancestors, we've inherited a world rich with a tapestry of life—an intricate web of biodiversity that sustains our very existence. As we progress deeper into the Anthropocene, the tenacity of our natural heritage hinges upon the decisions we make and the policies we implement. "Conserving the Web of Life: Policies for Preservation" is not merely a call to action; it's a blueprint for survival, a comprehensive plan to safeguard the genetic, species, and ecosystem diversity that form the cornerstones of our planet's resilience.

Habitat restoration emerges as a cornerstone of biodiversity preservation. It's not simply about bringing back what was once lost; it's about rekindling the dynamic processes that sustain ecosystems. This restoration often involves reforestation, wetland construction, and the removal of invasive species, which in turn helps to maintain crucial ecosystem services. Such practices are not just environmentally sound— they're economically imperative, for they bolster natural systems that purify our air and water, pollinate our crops, and protect our coastlines.

Protected areas serve as sanctuaries in this era of widespread habitat destruction. These are the bastions where nature is allowed to flourish, unimpeded by the indelible hand of human activities. Establishing national parks, wildlife reserves, and wilderness areas not only conserves habitats for endangered species, but also provides places where humans can reconnect with the natural world. The effectiveness of these zones, however, goes beyond their boundaries, as the bidirectional flow of ecological benefits can enrich the surrounding landscapes as well.

Conservation programs, both governmental and non-governmental, knit together the efforts of individuals and communities toward the protection and recovery of species under threat. Initiatives such as captive breeding, reintroduction programs, habitat corridors, and genetic rescue serve as lifeboats, ensuring populations remain viable. Coordinated actions under the umbrellas of these programs amplify conservation outcomes and contribute significantly to global biodiversity conservation efforts.

The Rights of Nature is a revolutionary concept that has gained traction, wherein legal personhood is granted to elements of the environment such as rivers, forests, and ecosystems. By embedding nature's rights into the legal framework, these policies embody an ethical paradigm that acknowledges nature's intrinsic value independent of human use, which is seminal in altering our interaction with the natural world.

International waters, encompassing nearly half of the Earth's surface, remain the least protected part of our planet. The High Seas Treaty, or Biodiversity Beyond National Jurisdiction Treaty, is aimed at filling this governance gap, providing the legal framework for establishing protected marine areas in the high seas and ensuring sustainable use of marine resources. This treaty symbolizes a momentous step toward global ocean stewardship, ensuring the wealth of biodiversity inhabiting the planet's most expansive biome is conserved for generations.

Global accords, such as the Convention on Biological Diversity (CBD) and the Paris Agreement, play a pivotal role by setting international standards and commitments to protect biodiversity. Such agreements mobilize nations to partake in concerted efforts in conservation, whether it's through the protection of critical habitats, sustainable utilization of natural resources, or integration of biodiversity considerations into policies and programs across sectors.

Transboundary conservation programs offer a glimpse into what collaboration across borders can achieve. The Great Limpopo Transfrontier Park, for example, links protected areas across South Africa, Mozambique, and Zimbabwe, allowing wildlife to roam freely across national borders. These collaborative efforts also alleviate the pressures of poaching, habitat loss, and species extinction by sharing resources and knowledge, ultimately bolstering regional biodiversity conservation.

For our policies to persevere, they must be as adaptive and resilient as the ecosystems they aim to protect. They should evolve alongside the shifting baselines of our changing world, with agility to respond to new challenges that emerge. This involves not only crafting wise policies but ensuring robust and transparent systems of governance to implement and monitor them effectively so that no backsliding on commitments can happen.

Our ambitions must also rise to meet the needs of local communities, embedding the ethos of sustainability and stewardship at the heart of cultural, economic, and political norms. A future in which conservation is a universal value, intuitive to our way of life, is possible. We hold the potential to be architects of a legacy that reveres and preserves the kaleidoscope of life on Earth.

As we weave the narrative of our time, let us choose a plot that honors the interdependent nature of life. For in conserving the web of life, we craft the story not just of survival, but of thriving—a tale in which each strand, from the humblest insect to the grandest forest, is acknowledged for its role in the symphony of existence.

Through our endeavors in habitat restoration, the establishment of protected areas, and the implementation of innovative conservation programs, we have the tools at our disposal. Invoking the rights of nature, we can instill a new legal ethic that respects the life force that pulses through our world. And by ratifying transformative international treaties such as the High Seas Treaty, we expand the domain of our stewardship beyond our immediate horizons.

In this crucial epoch, it is our shared duty to ensure policies for preservation become the foundation upon which we build a sustainable future. The vitality of our planet relies on our concerted efforts to uphold and expand upon the work laid before us. Let us muster the strength, the will, and the vision to embrace this ongoing challenge, so that the generations yet to come may marvel at the resplendence of life's diversity, unbridled and free-flowing as nature intended.

The Imperative for Biodiversity Integrity

Maintaining the integrity of biodiversity is not merely an environmentalist's pursuit; it is a fundamental necessity for the survival and well-being of all life on Earth. Throughout the preceding chapters, we've explored the myriad of ways human activity has impacted the planet. Now, we turn our attention to the urgent need to safeguard our natural heritage, a cornerstone of which is the vast tapestry of life forms—the biodiversity that sustains us and the ecosystems upon which we depend.

Biodiversity, the diversity within species, among species, and of ecosystems, serves as a wellspring for ecosystem resilience and flexibility. This biological variety enables life to persist through change and adversity, much like diversifying an investment portfolio to manage risk. And just like a robust financial portfolio, biodiversity's true value becomes most evident during times of crisis or change.

Our collective impact has been profound and, too often, adverse. Ecosystems worldwide are losing species at a rate estimated to be dozens to thousands of times higher than the natural background rate. Such loss erodes the resilience of ecosystems, diminishing their ability to provide the services we not only enjoy but require: clean air and water, pollination of crops, natural disease control, and the regulation of climate.

To turn the tide on biodiversity loss, we must adopt a holistic approach that addresses the drivers of this decline. These include habitat destruction, overexploitation of species, pollution, climate change, and invasive species. Each driver is a complex problem in itself, but they are interconnected, and our solutions must be as well.

Conservation biology offers us strategies for maintaining and recovering biodiversity. The creation of protected areas has been pivotal, allowing ecosystems and species to thrive without significant human interference. However, establishing such zones is just the beginning. They must be effectively managed, interconnected through ecological corridors, and supported by sustainable practices in the surrounding areas to ensure their efficacy.

Meanwhile, ecological restoration offers a proactive toolkit for repairing damaged ecosystems through enhancing their natural resilience and functionality. By reinstating native species, removing invasive ones, and rehabilitating landscapes, we can reforge the broken links in the chain of biodiversity.

Yet, the question must not be how can we protect the environment but how can we create a way of life that does not destroy it. Sustainable land-use practices, reimagining agriculture, urban planning that incorporates green spaces and biodiversity—these are challenges that demand not only environmental understanding, but also social ingenuity and political will.

Intrinsic to the struggle for biodiversity integrity is the necessity for equitable resource sharing. The benefits of conservation and sustainable use of biodiversity should be shared fairly and equitably, not hoarded by the few at the expense of the many. Inequity breeds not only poverty but resentment and conflict, which in turn stimulate the degradation of natural resources.

Education plays a crucial role in promoting biodiversity integrity. By raising public awareness about the values of biodiversity and the steps people can take to conserve and use it sustainably, we empower individuals and communities to take action. Every small choice and action contributes to a larger paradigm shift toward a world in which biodiversity is valued, protected, and wisely used.

The private sector also has a vital part to play, with green business models that prioritize sustainability and biodiversity protection offering avenues for positive change. Sustainable supply chains, reduced environmental footprints, and green consumer products aren't just good for the planet—they're increasingly demanded by consumers and can provide companies with a competitive edge.

And let's not forget technology's role; from biotechnology to remote sensing and data analytics, technological innovations can provide us with the tools to monitor, understand, and preserve biodiversity more effectively than ever before. These solutions, however, must be developed and applied thoughtfully; technology must be our servant in this endeavor, not our master.

Finally, political leadership and governance are critical. We need policies that integrate biodiversity considerations into all sectors of government and society. International agreements such as the Convention on Biological Diversity set the framework, but real change happens at the national and local levels, where laws are enacted, resources are allocated, and conservation measures take physical shape.

As we advocate for biodiversity integrity, it becomes evident that this quest is not just about saving other species; it's about preserving the possibilities for future generations of humanity. Our fates are bound together in a single, delicate web. By pulling on one thread, we send reverberations through the entire network—jeopardizing all it supports, ourselves included.

In conclusion, the imperative for biodiversity integrity is the imperative for our continued existence, prosperity, and well-being on this planet. Our natural heritage is not a luxury but a foundation. Let us then act with the urgency and dedication the defense of this cornerstone demands, knowing our legacy will be measured by the health of the world we leave behind.

Chapter 9:
Cultivating Tomorrow:
Seeds of Agricultural Innovation

As we've traversed the terrains of conservation and sustainable practices in previous chapters, the significance of reinventing agriculture as a bastion of innovation can't be overstressed. Within this chapter, we delve into the fecund grounds of agriculture, exploring how the synthesis of traditional wisdom and pioneering science leads to the propagation of sustainable methods that are vital for our food systems' resilience.

In the face of climate change, resource depletion, and a burgeoning global population, agriculture must adapt—employing strategies such as precision farming, biotechnology, and soil health enhancement to yield an abundant future. By integrating these ingenious farming practices, we emerge not just as cultivators of crops but stewards of an ecological legacy, ensuring a nutritious and secure food supply while respecting the very Earth that feeds us.

The meaningful transformation of our agricultural paradigms holds the promise of harmony between humanity and nature, an equilibrium that is both desirable and imperative for tomorrow's generations. And thus, we plant the seeds of agricultural innovation, germinating in the fertile soil of sustainability to grow an endurant world.

Comparing Cultivations: Sustainable Versus Conventional

Sustainable and conventional farming stand at a crossroads between legacy and innovation, with wide-reaching impacts on our environment, societies, and future food security. Deciphering their contrasts is pivotal for shaping our path to a sustainable world.

Conventional farming, the bedrock of the post-war agricultural boom, has long been propelled by monocultures, synthetic fertilizers, and chemical pesticides. It's buoyed by the intensive labor of machines and framed by economies that favor large-scale production. Indeed, this system has remarkably amplified food output, but not without collateral costs to the soil's vitality and ecosystems' balance.

Conversely, sustainable farming is a symphony of practices harmonizing with nature's rhythms. It treads lightly on the land, employing crop rotation, organic inputs, and conservation tillage. This agricultural ethos cherishes biodiversity, nurtures soil health, and embraces eco-friendly pest management.

Where conventional farming often views the soil as a mere medium for growth, sustainable farming upholds it as a complex, living ecosystem. Integrated pest management, cover crops, and agroforestry are sustainably farmed soil's cherished companions. They nourish a fertile cradle for diverse life by retaining water like a sponge and fostering robust crops less reliant on chemical inputs.

Water usage illustrates another stark contrast between conventional and sustainable farming. The conventional approach leans on liberal irrigation strategies and substantial surface water, sometimes leading to waterlogging, salinization, and aquifer depletion. In sustainable farming, water conservation is key. Drip irrigation, rainwater harvesting, and the judicious reuse of water course through its veins, threading the needle of efficiency and respect for this invaluable resource.

When examining energy consumption, it becomes apparent that conventional farming's appetite for fossil fuels is insatiable. It drives tractors, synthesizes fertilizers, and powers food processing. Despite its efficiency in output, it's entangled in a web of carbon emissions. Sustainable farming, in contrast, could be likened to a judicious energy gourmet, opting for renewable energy sources and reducing energy expenditure wherever feasible, lessening its climate footprint.

In pest management, conventional farming oft wields a chemical arsenal, an effective yet blunt instrument that risks collateral damage to non-target organisms and engenders resistance. Sustainable farming's strategy is more akin to a masterful chess game, deploying beneficial insects, crop diversity, and pheromone traps to outmaneuver pests.

One area conventional farming shines is in yield maximization, a testament to its engineering marvel. However, the long-term viability of this high-yield paradigm is clouded by soil degradation, water scarcity, and biodiversity decline. Sustainable agriculture may yield less per acre, but its long-term perspective seeks to balance productivity with environmental stewardship.

Economic implications stand at the heart of this debate. Conventional farming's scale economies can offer lower costs and higher outputs, which are essential for feeding a growing population. In contrast, sustainable farming often involves greater labor costs and potentially higher consumer prices. These numbers, however, don't account for the hidden costs—environmental degradation, health impacts from chemicals, and carbon emissions—that may not be immediately reflected in the price of food but are ultimately borne by society.

Market access and subsidies currently favor conventional farming, born from a legacy of post-war policies aimed at maximizing production. Sustainable farming, which requires a shift in policy frameworks and market dynamics, seeks to level the playing field through incentives for environmentally beneficial practices.

Consumer awareness and demand also play a crucial role. The growing appetite for organic and locally sourced food illuminates a shifting paradigm in which the ecological footprint of one's diet becomes as much a personal health choice as a planetary one.

Climate change resilience adds another layer to the scales. Sustainable farming practices can enhance adaptability to extreme weather events through biodiversity and soil health. Conventional farming's reliance on narrow genetic bases and exposed monocultures could falter due to climatic volatility.

Innovation in sustainable agriculture continues to flourish, from precision farming technologies that optimize resource use to the integration of agroecological principles into mainstream farming operations. An evolution in scientific understanding and technology aids sustainable farming in narrowing the yield gap while bolstering its environmental credentials.

Ultimately, transitioning from conventional to sustainable farming isn't a binary switch but a spectrum of practices, each with its trade-offs and potentials for agriculture's future landscape. A mosaic of both methods may emerge, borrowing the strengths of each to weave a new narrative of productivity coexisting with the planet's well-being.

As we stand at the intersection of human need and environmental imperatives, comparing sustainable versus conventional farming is not merely academic. It invites us to chart a course in our agricultural practices that embodies respect for the Earth, foresight for future generations, and the wisdom to realize our food systems can be as regenerative as the nature from which they spring. As global citizens, it's our shared responsibility to embrace this transformative vision for agriculture—a vision not just of survival but of thriving in symbiosis with our living world.

Embracing Ecological Farming Practices: From Organic Farming to Agroforestry

The horizon of agriculture is being reshaped by the pressing need for sustainability, giving rise to practices that harmonize with nature's rhythms. At the forefront of this transformation lies organic farming and agroforestry—methods that not only offer a reprieve to the stressed planet, but also promise renewed productivity and ecosystem health.

Organic farming eschews synthetic chemicals, nurturing soils with organic matter and adopting natural pest control, thus, strengthening the biodiversity upon which our food systems hinge. Agroforestry, an ancestral wisdom now taking root in modern soil, interlaces crops with trees to create symbiotic guilds, reducing the need for artificial inputs and bolstering resilience against climate extremes. This embrace of ecological farming practices is a testament to agriculture's adaptive spirit and highlights the regenerative potential embedded in the marriage of traditional knowledge and contemporary science.

Greening the Fields: Eco-Farming Initiatives

Within the tapestry of sustainability, agriculture holds a significant thread. It's the nexus where human need intersects with the ecological integrity of our planet. How we cultivate our food can tip the balance toward either degradation or regeneration. Let's explore the harmonious practices that can sustain and nourish not just our bodies but the very Earth itself. Embracing ecological farm practices extends beyond traditional methods to incorporating innovative approaches that respect natural processes and enhance biodiversity.

Organic farming is one of the most recognized forms of agriculture rooted in ecological principles. At its core, it shuns synthetic pesticides and fertilizers, relying instead on natural substances and processes. This approach supports soil health, conserves water, and protects wildlife. Farmers who adopt these practices contribute to the long-term sustainability of agriculture by maintaining soil fertility and promoting environmental stability.

Conservation agriculture is another crucial practice in the ecological farming spectrum. It's a three-pronged approach focusing on minimizing soil disturbance (no-tillage), maintaining permanent soil cover, and diversifying crop species in rotations and associations. According to the

Food and Agriculture Organization, conservation agriculture improves soil structure, enhances biodiversity, and reduces the carbon footprint.

Biodynamic agriculture goes a step further. It views the farm as a cohesive, interconnected organism. This method extends beyond organic farming by incorporating specific preparations made from herbs, minerals, and manures, and is aligned with cosmic rhythms. Biodynamic practices have been shown to produce robust, resilient farms that can weather environmental stresses.

Reduced tillage, a component of conservation agriculture, minimizes soil disruption. Studies have shown reduced tillage can increase water infiltration and retention, reduce erosion, and build organic soil matter, contributing to the sequestration of carbon in the soil.

Meanwhile, precision agriculture employs technology to optimize field-level management with respect to crop farming. It involves the use of sensors, satellite imagery, and data analytics to enhance efficiency and reduce waste. Precision techniques can minimize the use of water, fertilizers, and pesticides, leading to less environmental impact while maintaining or even improving yields.

Another component vital to ecological farming is Integrated Pest Management (IPM). IPM uses a combination of biological, cultural, mechanical, and chemical methods in a synchronized manner to manage pests with the least possible harm to people, property, and the environment. It emphasizes the growth of a healthy crop with the least possible disruption to agro-ecosystems and encourages natural pest control mechanisms.

Sustainable livestock management intertwines with these crop-based practices. It involves rotational grazing in which livestock move between pastures to allow regrowth of vegetation. This procedure mimics natural grazing patterns, improves animal health, reduces reliance on feed, builds soil health, and improves the nutrient cycle within the farm ecosystem.

These ecological farming practices don't exist in isolation; they are interconnected. Organic methods serve as the foundation, naturally supporting IPM and biodynamic approaches. Conservation agriculture complements reduced tillage, preserving soil structure and moisture. Precision agriculture, meanwhile, provides overarching support through technology, enhancing efficiency across all farming methods.

In assuming these ecological practices, farmers play a critical role in addressing some of the most pressing global challenges. They help mitigate climate change by sequestering carbon in the soil, foster biodiversity, reduce pollution and water use, and contribute to building resilient food systems.

The transition to ecological farming practices requires a paradigm shift—a move away from seeing farms as mere food factories toward recognizing them as living systems that are integral parts of our global ecological network. It involves understanding dynamics from soil microbiota to pollinators and from water cycles to carbon flows.

Supporting this transition are various incentives and certifications such as the Organic, Biodynamic, and Rainforest Alliance, which help guide consumers in their choices and promote ecological farming methods. Moreover, these practices often yield products that command a premium in the market and can improve farmer livelihoods.

The benefits of ecological farming practices are irrefutable, and their adoption is a critical step toward sustainable agriculture. By fostering practices that conserve and enhance our natural resources, we can chart a course that feeds our growing population while safeguarding the environment for future generations.

Together, these practices form the backbone of a revolution in agriculture that aligns farming with natural ecological processes. They are pathways toward healing a world too often scarred by our consumption and disregard for the intricate balance that sustains us. Every seed sown in this manner is an investment in a future in which nature and humanity can thrive in symphony.

By embracing ecological farm practices, we are not merely cultivating land; we are nurturing a worldview. This shift is fundamental to the larger transformation highlighted throughout this volume, weaving agriculture into the very fabric of a sustainable future. The transformative power of these practices may be our most profound and promising means of restoring balance to our beleaguered planet.

Indigenous Agricultural Methods and Practices

As we traverse the pioneering ideals of ecological farming in this pivotal chapter, it's essential to acknowledge the profound wisdom carved out across millennia by the world's Indigenous cultures. Time-honored agricultural practices developed by ancient communities aren't just cultural artifacts; they are blueprints of sustainable living and farming that are experiencing a renewal in today's shift toward environmental stewardship. Agroecology, a movement at the forefront of which is the merger of agronomic science with ecological sustainability, finds many of its roots entwined with the ancient ways of Indigenous peoples.

Centuries before modern terminology caught up, Indigenous communities executed the principles of agroecology through their intimate understanding of local ecosystems. Their practices emphasized the importance of nurturing a symbiotic relationship between crops and their environment and employed techniques that enhanced biodiversity and enriched soils without the need for chemical interventions. Such methods provide valuable insights into natural pest management and agricultural resilience, proving fundamental to modern agroecological applications.

Agroforestry, another age-old practice, cleverly combines agriculture with the thoughtful preservation of trees and shrubs. It enhances the resilience of an ecosystem by protecting soils from erosion, improving water cycles, and providing a habitat for a multitude of species. Indigenous agroforestry practices are not only an inspiration but a direct model for contemporary land management strategies aiming to heal damaged ecosystems while producing food sustainably.

The principles of permaculture also borrow heavily from the methods refined by Indigenous cultures. By designing agricultural systems that mimic natural ecosystems, permaculture achieves sustainability principles such as self-sufficiency, biodiversity, and resource conservation. Ancestral land use strategies inform its ethics and design principles, which are fundamental in creating balanced and productive landscapes that require minimal input to maintain.

Transhumant pastoralism (THP) is an ancient and dynamic practice in which herders move livestock according to seasonal rhythms, tapping into the diversity of ecosystems to sustain their herds. This practice supports biodiversity, aids in the management of wildfires and brushwood expansion, and nurtures grasslands through natural fertilization. As the world grapples with developing sustainable livestock management systems, THP provides lessons in how low-impact herding can harmoniously exist within diverse ecosystems.

Inherent to Indigenous agriculture is the concept of crop rotation, which, when practiced, bolsters soil fertility and disrupts pest and disease cycles. The knowledge of rotating plant families and allowing periods of fallow is deeply embedded in these traditional systems. Contemporary sustainable agriculture is reviving these practices in order to reduce dependency on synthetic fertilizers and build soil health.

Cover cropping, another practice inherited from ancestors, entails growing specific crops primarily for soil protection and enhancement. Modern regenerative agriculture is learning from these practices to prevent soil erosion, manage water, enhance organic matter, and promote beneficial insect populations—all integral parts of maintaining a healthy agroecosystem.

The technique of intercropping and cultivating polycultures— growing multiple crops in proximity—creates a complex habitat that deters pests and diseases through natural means. By fostering polycultures, Indigenous farmers managed to grow a diverse food supply that was less susceptible to catastrophic loss. This practice informs modern techniques aimed at enhancing the resilience and productivity of crop systems in the face of climatic challenges.

Water harvesting techniques, ingeniously developed by Indigenous cultures, encompass an array of practices from simple rainwater catchments to sophisticated irrigation systems. These practices maximize the use of available water resources, mitigate the impacts of droughts, and demonstrate water's precious nature. They have inspired current sustainable water management practices, especially critical in areas where water scarcity poses a significant challenge.

Practiced for centuries by Indigenous communities, Integrated Agriculture-Aquaculture (IAA) is a tradition in which the waste from fish or other aquatic animals provides nutrients for plants, and the plants, in turn, help purify water for the fish. This closed-loop system has been popularized today as aquaponics and is being hailed as a highly efficient method to produce both fish and vegetables with minimal waste.

Every one of these Indigenous agricultural methods carries a stem of knowledge that can inspire and guide a more sustainable way of living. They're not just instructional; they are warrant to the sophistication and foresight of ancient cultures that understood the importance of living in harmony with the Earth. Embracing these time-tested practices offers more than a nod to the past; it presents a clear and actionable pathway for our journey toward sustainable agriculture and ecosystem management. The ingenuity of Indigenous methods, when applied with modern understanding, yields a powerful synergy to advance our quest for agricultural methods that are not only productive, but also genuinely regenerative.

Integrating these practices into the pulse of modern agriculture involves consciously weaving the threads of ancestral wisdom into the fabric of contemporary farming systems. By investing in research that explores and validates these practices, policymakers and practitioners can craft strategies that pair historical reverence with scientific innovation. The lessons from Indigenous agricultural methods and practices transcend mere techniques; they embody an ethos of reciprocity with the land and an understanding that when we care for the systems that sustain us, they, in turn, provide abundance.

Through the earnest revival of these practices, we are provided the tools to repair our relationship with the planet and to nurture its resources rather than deplete them. As this chapter unfolds, remember the importance of looking backward to ancient principles to inform our forward motion. For the seeds of our future sustainability germinate in the roots of traditional knowledge.

The Sustainable Food Equation

Within agricultural innovation, the thread that seems most vibrant is the concept of the sustainable food equation. This equation isn't merely arithmetic or economics—it's a blend of science, ethics, and pragmatism. It approaches food production not just as a means of sustenance but as a holistic practice that affects our environmental, social, and economic fabrics.

The essence of this equation is the balancing of the inputs and outputs of our agricultural systems in such a way we can feed our growing population without depleting natural resources or causing irreversible environmental damage. It's a delicate balancing act that requires deep consideration of the interplay among land use, water availability, energy consumption, biodiversity, and human labor.

At the heart of creating a sustainable food system is soil health. Rich, fertile soil teeming with life is the foundation of robust ecosystems and productive farms. Practices such as crop rotation, cover cropping, and reduced tillage help to maintain soil structure, prevent erosion, and build organic matter, which are all key to long-term sustainability.

Water is another critical piece of the equation. Sustainable farming practices aim to use water efficiently while maintaining the health of aquatic ecosystems. Techniques such as drip irrigation and rainwater harvesting can substantially reduce the amount of water required for crop production.

Energy usage in agriculture is a complex issue, as traditional farming is often reliant on fossil fuels. The sustainable food equation seeks to integrate renewable energy sources—such as solar or wind power—to mitigate the carbon footprint associated with food production.

Biodiversity is an ally in sustainable agriculture. Diverse systems are more resilient and productive and foster a range of ecosystem services, such as pest control, pollination, and disease regulation. Preserving genetic diversity in crop species and their wild counterparts allows for adaptive management in the face of climate change.

Food waste is a significant issue that the sustainable food equation aims to solve through better supply chain management and consumer practices. Reducing waste not only conserves the energy and resources invested in producing food, but also decreases greenhouse gas emissions from decomposing organic matter in landfills.

Local food systems bring multiple benefits to the sustainable food equation. They shorten supply chains, reduce transportation emissions, and support local economies. Furthermore, they can encourage seasonal eating and promote diversity in diets and farming systems.

Technological advances play a crucial role in this equation. Precision agriculture, for instance, uses data and technology to make farming more accurate and resource-efficient. Innovations in biotechnology such as drought-resistant crops may also contribute to sustainability, though they are accompanied by ethical and ecological considerations that must be thoughtfully addressed.

Labor practices intersect with the food equation through the lens of social sustainability. Fair labor conditions, equitable economic opportunities, and community engagement are indispensable components of a sustainable food system. Empowering smallholder farmers and recognizing the rights of farmworkers are as critical as environmental stewardship.

Consumer choices—what we eat, how much we consume, and our level of waste—are integral to the equation. Sustainable diets, characterized by low-environmental impact foods and mindful consumption patterns, can significantly mitigate the toll on natural resources.

Policy frameworks must underpin and facilitate all aspects of the sustainable food equation. Regulations and incentives can drive adoption of sustainable practices, support research and innovation, and help to integrate sustainability principles into both local and global markets.

Ultimately, the sustainable food equation isn't static; it's a dynamic system that evolves with human knowledge and natural cycles. It demands active engagement and continuous adaptation. The promise of such an equation is not only a sustainable food system but a resilient and equitable one that nourishes both people and the planet.

Our ability to solve the sustainable food equation will depend on collaboration across disciplines and sectors, embracing both ancient wisdom and modern innovation. It will require the collective will to reimagine and reconstruct our agriculture systems based on the principles of sustainability—principles that ensure the longevity not just of human populations but of the soils, waters, and biodiversity that sustain us all.

Plowing Through Challenges: Agriculture at a Crossroads

As the narrative of sustainability unfolds, agriculture stands at an epic intersection. The path ahead is riddled with challenges that demand not just attention but immediate and decisive action. This section delves into the intricate web of difficulties facing today's agricultural sector and envisions pathways to overcome them, an accomplishment necessary to our pursuit of a sustainable future.

Modern agriculture is shouldered with the monumental task of feeding an ever-growing population while wrestling with limited natural resources. Despite technological advancements in farming practices, the environmental toll is stark. Our soil, the very mantle of agriculture, is degrading at an alarming rate due to intensive farming, deforestation for agricultural expansion, and erosion. Overcoming these soil health issues is crucial for the sustainability of our food systems.

Water scarcity is another formidable challenge agriculture faces. Nonoptimized irrigation practices lead to the wastage of precious water resources. At the same time, contamination from pesticides and fertilizers pollutes water bodies, harming aquatic life and reducing the availability of clean water.

The use of agrochemicals, fertilizers, and pesticides in traditional farming practices has escalated concerns about health implications, biodiversity loss, and the disruption of ecosystems. The delicate balance of nature is often tipped off kilter when these substances leach into the surrounding environment, causing harm to pollinators, beneficial insects, and soil microbiomes that are essential to agricultural resilience.

Climate change stands as a menacing backdrop to these issues, altering weather patterns and exacerbating existing vulnerabilities. Extreme weather events, fluctuations in temperatures, and shifting seasons lead to crop failures and make pests and diseases more difficult to manage.

One of the most scathing critiques of current agricultural practices is their contribution to greenhouse gas (GHG) emissions. The carbon footprint from synthetic fertilizer production, methane release from livestock, and deforestation are major factors in global warming, placing agriculture in direct conflict with climate mitigation efforts.

Social and economic challenges also shape the agricultural landscape. Smallholder farmers often lack access to markets, credit, and technology that could improve their livelihoods and enable sustainable practices. Moreover, they are particularly vulnerable to fluctuations in the market and climate impacts due to their marginal operational scale and resources.

Addressing these multifaceted challenges requires an integrative approach that combines innovation, policy, and community engagement. Sustainable agricultural practices such as crop rotation, conservation tillage, integrated pest management, and organic farming can enhance soil health, reduce dependency on chemical inputs, and increase resilience to climate change.

Advancements in precision agriculture can help optimize water and fertilizer use, thus, conserving resources and minimizing environmental impacts. These technologies, when harnessed responsibly, have the potential to drastically improve farming efficiency and reduce wastage.

Genetic improvements in crops are another avenue being explored to enhance resistance to pests, diseases, and environmental stresses. However, the ethical and ecological implications of such modifications need careful consideration to ensure biodiversity conservation and public acceptance.

Farmers' access to markets, credit, and information can be improved with better networks and support systems. Cooperatives, community-supported agriculture, and fair-trade movements are vital in empowering farmers and ensuring the consumers' demand for sustainably produced food is met.

Public policies play a foundational role in shaping a sustainable agricultural future. Subsidies and incentives aligned with environmentally friendly practices can encourage farmers to transition toward more sustainable methods. Moreover, policies need to safeguard the rights and welfare of farmers and rural communities, ensuring they are pivotal stakeholders in the sustainability narrative.

Ultimately, a shift in cultural attitudes toward food and farming is indispensable. Consumers hold power in their preferences and purchasing behavior. Solidarity behind sustainable initiatives and informed choices can drive the demand for sustainable produce, fostering a culture of responsible consumption and production.

The current standing of agriculture beckons a profound reflection on how we value the sources of our sustenance and a redefinition of what progress in agriculture looks like. It is about securing food for our future generations while nurturing the planet that has nourished us so far. As daunting as the challenges to this are, they are not insurmountable, given our capacity for innovation and cooperation.

Future of Agriculture: Sustainable Perspectives

Today, the agricultural sector stands at an important crossroads. The necessity for increased food production to meet the demands of a growing global population is tempered by the imperative to do so sustainably. As we gaze into the agrarian horizon, we must recognize the essential interplay between the environment and human stewardship in kindling the dawn of a sustainable future for agriculture.

Sustainability in farming hinges on methods that harmoniously blend economic viability with environmental health and social responsibility. It rests on the adoption of agricultural practices that not only increase productivity and resilience, but also reduce the environmental footprint and enhance the well-being of farmers and their communities.

One promising factor is innovative farming techniques, such as precision agriculture, which employs information technology and a range of items such as GPS guidance, control systems, sensors, robotics, drones, autonomous vehicles, variable rate technology, and automated hardware. This suite of innovations can optimize field-level management with regard to crop farming. By precisely managing soil amendments and utilizing inputs such as water and fertilizer, precision agriculture can vastly increase efficiency and reduce waste.

Regenerative agriculture is another revolutionary practice. It focuses on topsoil regeneration, increasing biodiversity, improving the water cycle, and supporting biosequestration, thereby enhancing ecosystem services. By revitalizing soil health through practices such as crop rotation, cover cropping, and no-till farming, regenerative methods work to increase soil organic matter, which in turn improves agricultural yields and resilience to climate variability.

Integrated pest management (IPM)—a sustainable approach to pest control—combines biological, cultural, physical, and chemical tools in a way that minimizes economic, health, and environmental risks. IPM emphasizes the growth of a healthy crop with the least possible disruption to agro-ecosystems, encouraging the natural pest control mechanisms inherent in them.

The reintegration of livestock and crops in a more cyclical and synergistic fashion—something that has fallen out of favor in industrial agriculture—could also mark a return to more sustainable methods. Agroecological practices that intertwine cropping and animal husbandry have the potential to create self-sustaining systems that recycle nutrients and improve soil fertility without heavy reliance on synthetic inputs.

Hydroponics and aquaponics are modern agricultural systems that embody sustainability by reducing the need for soil and significantly lowering water usage. These systems can be employed in urban environments, thus, decreasing the distance food travels from farm to consumer and contributing to the reduction of greenhouse gas emissions associated with transport.

Community-supported agriculture (CSA) and urban farming initiatives provide alternative, sustainable means of food production and distribution. These models rebuild the connection between farmers and consumers and foster local economies. They enable consumers to share in the risk and reward of food production, promoting transparency and resilience in food systems.

Meanwhile, the expansion of genetically modified organisms (GMOs) has stirred a robust debate. Advocates argue that GMOs can help to sustainably increase crop yields and resilience, whereas opponents raise concerns over environmental impacts and corporate control over seeds and biodiversity. The future of sustainable agriculture may hinge upon the ability to navigate this complex issue with scientific integrity and ethical foresight.

Sustainable agriculture also requires a commitment to nurturing agrobiodiversity—the variety and variability of animals, plants, and microorganisms used directly or indirectly for food and agriculture. Protecting this diversity ensures a wider gene pool, which enables adaptation to changing environments and pest and disease pressures—a quintessential attribute for the resilience of food systems.

Education and extension services are paramount in the transition toward sustainable farming practices. By empowering farmers with knowledge and techniques that enhance sustainability, communities can be equipped to embrace innovation while preserving the traditional wisdom that has sustained generations.

Smart policies and governance are indispensable in spearheading a sustainable agricultural transformation. Governments and institutions must craft policies that incentivize regenerative, low-impact farming, support local food systems, provide for robust research and extension services, and aid in the transition for farmers moving away from conventional practices.

One of the overarching themes in the realm of sustainable agriculture is the reality of a changing climate. Agricultural systems must be designed and managed in ways that not only mitigate climate change by reducing emissions, but also adapt to the increasing variability in weather patterns. This challenges us to not only envision but also to execute a pragmatic yet visionary approach to our food systems, embedding resilience at their core.

In the journey ahead, the synergy between technological advancements and time-honored sustainable practices will likely define the future of agriculture. From biotech to agroecology and from data analytics to permaculture, the integration of diverse approaches can pave the way for a farming future that is as productive as it is sustainable.

Finally, this sustainable shift also requires societal transformation. It calls for consumers to be not merely passive purchasers but active participants in a food system committed to nourishing both people and the planet. The food choices made today by millions will collectively shape the agricultural landscapes of tomorrow.

In conclusion, the future of agriculture isn't merely about producing more—it's about doing so in a way that aligns with the planet's natural rhythms, meets human needs, and honors the integrity of both current and future generations. As we stand on the frontier of innovations and opportunities, we must challenge ourselves to think creatively, act courageously, and farm sustainably, for therein lies the promise of tomorrow's harvest.

Chapter 10:
New Horizons:
Technological Frontiers in Sustainability

"New Horizons: Technological Frontiers in Sustainability" teems with optimism and innovation as it delves into highlighting the integral role of technology in steering our society toward a sustainable future. Advancements in this area offer a beacon of hope, shining light on new pathways for mitigating environmental impacts and fostering a symbiosis between progress and preservation.

The realm of sustainability technology is not just about creating gadgets and gizmos—it's about redefining our relationship with the planet. Groundbreaking developments in fields such as renewable energy storage, biodegradable materials, precision agriculture, and smart urban planning are already setting the stage for a more resilient world. These technological strides, paired with a steadfast commitment to ethics, can transform challenges into stepping-stones toward enduring solutions.

Our journey in this chapter affirms sustainability isn't merely about the resources we safeguard but the future we're courageous enough to imagine and build with every tool at our command.

Technological Potential in Sustainability: An Overview

As dawn breaks on the landscape of sustainability, technology stands as a beacon of hope; its luminescent promise touching every facet of human endeavor. At the intersection of innovation and environmentalism, technological potential is not just an asset but a necessity for envisioning a sustainable future. It's a canvas on which solutions to our pressing ecological challenges can be designed, tested, and implemented.

In this era of profound change, we find ourselves at a critical juncture. The technologies that once drove the juggernaut of industrialization, along with its heavy environmental cost, are being reevaluated and reshaped. We're steering toward an era where they serve as catalysts for regeneration, restoration, and resilience. This transition underscores a pivotal moment in history: the alignment of technological evolution with environmental stewardship.

In the realm of energy, the tapestry of innovation weaves new patterns. Renewable energy technologies such as wind turbines, solar panels, and hydropower are undergoing rapid advancement. They're becoming more efficient, more affordable, and more integrated into the very grid that powers our daily lives. The quest for storage solutions—key to addressing the intermittent nature of renewables—sees batteries growing in capacity and decreasing in price, setting the stage for a truly decentralized energy future.

In agriculture, technology is reshaping practices that, for too long, have been unsustainable. Precision agriculture harnesses the power of big data, artificial intelligence (AI), and the Internet of Things (IoT) to apply resources—water, fertilizers, and pesticides—more judiciously. Doing so reduces waste, minimizes environmental impacts, and boosts yields to feed a growing population.

The water crisis, a specter that looms large on the horizon of many communities, is being tackled with innovative desalination techniques, efficient purification systems, and smart water management tools. These technological advancements don't just promise access to clean water; they offer resilience against drought and water scarcity in an ever-more-volatile climate.

When it comes to waste, the technological horizon is brimming with transformative potential. The circular economy, powered by advancements in material science and recycling technologies, envisions a world where waste is not an endpoint but a resource—creating a loop that continually feeds into itself. This seismic shift could redefine consumption and production patterns, significantly reducing our ecological footprint.

Even our oceans, vast and often considered unreachable, are subject to the benevolent reach of technology. Autonomous underwater vehicles, remote sensing, and satellite technologies are granting us unprecedented insight into maritime ecosystems. These innovations allow for more informed conservation strategies and a deeper understanding of how oceans drive global systems, including climate.

Crucially, the technological potential in sustainability extends beyond hardware to include software, systems thinking, and process innovation. Smart grids, for instance, are revolutionizing how electricity is distributed and managed, leading to more resilient energy systems. Similarly, city planning tools empowered by big data analytics can lead to the development of greener, more sustainable urban environments.

Moreover, technology is cultivating collaboration across all levels, from local communities to global networks. Platforms for sharing information and fostering partnerships, such as the United Nations' Sustainable Development Goals (SDGs) initiatives, are accelerating the diffusion of sustainable technologies across borders and barriers.

However, it would be naive to assume the road to technological transformation is without bumps. The very act of innovation requires resources—materials, energy, human capital—which may in themselves pose sustainability challenges. Reducing the environmental impact of technology's life cycle, from cradle to grave, is a critical avenue for research and development.

Indeed, the barriers to harnessing technological potential are not solely technological themselves but often social, economic, and political. The diffusion of sustainable technologies into mainstream use depends on supportive policies, market mechanisms, and societal acceptance.

It's important to recognize technology doesn't operate in a vacuum. Its development and deployment are deeply entwined with human values, aspirations, and ingenuity. The harnessing of technological potential in sustainability is as much about the technology itself as it is about fostering a culture that embraces innovation for the common good.

In the journey toward a sustainable future, it's crucial to adopt an inclusive approach. Technological solutions must consider the needs of all stakeholders, particularly marginalized communities, ensuring the benefits of innovation don't perpetuate existing inequalities but rather ameliorate them.

Environmental monitoring, essential for understanding the health of our planet, has been invigorated by technology. Remote sensing and precision mapping allow us not only to witness the symptoms of ecological degradation but to diagnose the underlying conditions. Such capabilities are invaluable in forging targeted and timely interventions.

As we traverse this terrain of technological wonder, it's essential to remember technology is a tool in the hands of humanity. Its potential in sustainability is boundless, constrained only by our creativity, our commitment, and our will to ensure a harmonious coexistence with the world that sustains us. Let's bear in mind what we create with our minds and build with our hands can either heal or harm. The choice lies before us, as stewards of a world brimming with life, to ignite the spark of innovation for a sustainable legacy.

It's within this space we explore the grand narrative of technological potential in sustainability—an epic saga of human intellect, compassion, and foresight, woven into the tableau of ecological balance. And as the pages of this story unfurl, we capture the essence of sustainability itself: a symphony of collaborative progress, echoing through the annals of time toward a future we choose to create.

Ethical Considerations: Balancing Morality and Innovation

In the quest for sustainability, it's essential to not only consider the technological prowess, but also the ethical implications of our actions. As we delve into new technological frontiers, we often face novel challenges that interweave morality and innovation in complex ways. Unprecedented capabilities raise pivotal questions: Who benefits from these technologies, and at what cost?

The allure of technology in enhancing sustainability is undeniable. Advances in renewable energy, biotechnology, and environmental engineering promise a brighter future. Nonetheless, we must tread cautiously, ensuring our innovations align with ethical standards and prioritizing the well-being of both people and the planet.

While technological breakthroughs can mitigate climate change, reduce waste, and conserve resources, they can also lead to unintended consequences. Consider the dilemma of energy production technologies: While they have the potential to reduce greenhouse gas emissions, their manufacture and disposal can pose threats to both the environment and communities.

Similarly, the deployment of cutting-edge agricultural technologies must be considered through an ethical lens. The adoption of genetically modified organisms (GMOs), for instance, raises significant questions regarding biodiversity, food sovereignty, and long-term ecological impact.

The digital realm presents another area where ethical considerations intersect with sustainability innovation. The rise of big data and artificial intelligence (AI) offers powerful tools for environmental monitoring and decision-making. However, we must vigilantly address concerns related to privacy, equity, and algorithmic biases that may perpetuate existing disparities.

Furthermore, the distribution of technology's benefits and burdens must be equitable to ensure a just transition toward a sustainable future.

Socioeconomic disparities can be exacerbated if access to green technologies remains limited to affluent societies, leaving behind vulnerable populations that may bear the environmental brunt of others' technological advancements.

Fostering community involvement in the development and application of sustainable technologies can help bridge this ethical divide. Empowering communities to have a voice in technological choices ensures their needs and values are reflected in environmental solutions, fostering ownership and resilience.

Technological innovation must slide in lockstep with conserving traditional knowledge and practices. Indigenous wisdom, cultivated over millennia, can offer insights into living harmoniously with nature that should be respected and integrated into modern sustainability efforts.

The ethical use of natural resources in technology creation is yet another critical consideration. The extraction of rare earth minerals for renewable energy technologies, for example, must be scrutinized for its social and ecological footprint. Striking a balance between resource utilization and conservation is imperative to avoid repeating the destructive cycles of the past.

As we advance into novel ecological territories, bioethics provides a cornerstone for evaluating our actions' moral dimensions. It compels us to ask complex questions: How do we draw the line between ecological manipulation and restoration? What are the moral implications of altering ecosystems through technologies such as geoengineering?

The precautionary principle suggests when an activity raises threats of harm to human health or the environment, precautionary measures should be taken even if some cause-and-effect relationships are not scientifically established. This principle should guide the innovation process, ensuring we do not rush headlong into technological applications without due diligence regarding potential risks.

Standard setting and regulation play pivotal roles in navigating the ethical landscape of sustainability technology. Clear guidelines and robust oversight can ensure advancements align with societal values and environmental imperatives.

Moreover, the role of education in crafting an ethically conscious mindset toward sustainability cannot be overstated. By infusing curriculums with environmental ethics and interdisciplinary approaches, we can cultivate generations of innovators who are grounded in a moral compass that guides their scientific pursuits.

Finally, fostering global collaboration is crucial when considering the ethical implications of technological advancements. Sustainability challenges do not recognize borders, and neither should our ethical considerations. A collaborative approach can help to develop globally accepted standards and regulations that recognize the interconnected fabric of our planet's ecosystems and societies.

As we navigate the intricate path of integrating technological prowess with ethical responsibility, we pave the way for a more sustainable, equitable, and conscientious future. A future in which innovation thrives, but not at the expense of our moral obligations to protect and cherish the world we inhabit.

Future Breakthroughs: Technology's Role in Environmental Solutions

As we gaze toward the horizons of sustainability, technology gleams with the promise of environmental salvation. At the intersection where human ingenuity meets ecological necessity, we find ourselves speculating the shape of tomorrow. The forthcoming technological breakthroughs aren't merely hopeful projections—they're essential milestones on our path to a resilient planet.

High Among these anticipated triumphs is the development of carbon capture and storage (CCS) at a global scale. Past efforts have been stifled by cost and complexity, but disruptive innovations in this space could pivot the trajectory of our climatic future. Pioneering methods of carbon sequestration may soon enable us to extract greenhouse gases directly from the air, negating decades of industrial emissions.

Another promising avenue is the realm of energy storage. As we orient away from fossil fuels and embrace renewable sources, we're confronted by the intermittent nature of solar and wind power. Advanced battery technologies that are capable of storing vast amounts of energy for longer periods could emancipate our grid from these constraints, ensuring a consistent and reliable flow of green energy.

The sanctity of water remains a paramount concern as we brave the challenges ahead. The fusion of nanotechnology and biotechnology heralds the next generation of water purification systems, which could revolutionize access to clean water around the globe. These systems not only strive for efficiency, but also for the reduction of their own environmental footprints.

Urban agriculture is set to transform cityscapes into lush, productive landscapes. Vertical farms, which utilize hydroponics and aeroponics, not only defy the spatial limitations of traditional farming, but also minimize water usage and transport-related emissions. The smart integration of these agricultural innovations could render the metropolis a surprising bastion of sustainability.

In the vastness of our oceans, technology is charting unprecedented territories. Remote sensing and AI are converging to create sophisticated monitoring systems for marine ecosystems. Through these eyes in the sky—and below the waves—we'll unlock deeper understandings of oceanic health, breeding interventions that are precise and prescient.

Waste, the byproduct of our consumerist society, is due for a transformative reckoning. The circular economy, supported by technology, aspires to relegitimize the value in our discards. Through advanced sorting and recycling processes, even the most intractable materials could re-enter the cycle of use, challenging the very notion of waste itself.

Biodiversity conservation is primed to benefit from genomic technologies. The meticulous mapping and gene editing capabilities on the horizon afford us the means to strengthen ecosystems against the tide of extinction. Beyond that, they offer us the keys to resuscitating the genetic diversity that has slipped from our grasp.

The agricultural front will witness a series of surges as precision farming takes root. Coupled with big data and drone technology, future farms will be bastions of efficiency—boasting optimal outputs with minimal inputs. Smart farming can drastically reduce chemical usage, tailor water needs to precise requirements, and predict crop health and yields with astounding accuracy.

Transportation, a significant contributor to our environmental woes, is on the cusp of a sustainable revolution. The accelerated development of electric vehicles, fueled by forever-improving battery life and complemented by a burgeoning infrastructure, is already reshaping our roads. Autonomous vehicle technology promises to optimize fuel efficiency and reduce traffic congestion, which will lead to a cleaner atmosphere.

In the quest for sustainable materials, the synthesis of biodegradable composites breaks the reliance on environmentally taxing inputs. Innovations in material science can spawn products that meld into natural cycles at the end of their usefulness, gracefully decomposing without a trace of toxicity.

The digital realm offers a less tangible, yet equally critical, frontier for sustainability. The proliferation of sensors and the Internet of Things (IoT) endows our environments with a nervous system capable of detecting and responding to ecological changes. Data becomes a beacon, guiding our decisions and sharpening our response to environmental needs.

Renewable energy itself will see a cascade of advancements. Emerging technologies such as tidal and wave power could harness the inexhaustible energy of our seas. Meanwhile, ongoing improvements in solar panel efficiency portend a future in which solar becomes the cheapest and most abundant energy source worldwide.

Perhaps most auspicious are the innovations sparking at the confluence of multiple fields. Interdisciplinary efforts in AI, biotechnology, materials science, and more are fermenting solutions that outstrip the sum of their parts—a true testament to the collaborative spirit sustainability demands.

Throughout this ascendant era of technological potential, a caveat persists: as we harness these tools for environmental benefit, we must tread with ethical care and remain mindful of the implications on society and nature alike. In this balance, we'll find the wisdom to cultivate a world that flourishes not just through technological might, but through the harmonious interplay of life in all its forms.

Chapter 11:
Weaving the Threads:
Co-Creating Tomorrow's Sustainability

As we stand on the precipice of an epoch defined by unparalleled environmental change, both alarming and hopeful, the synthesis of knowledge across our shared disciplines paints a clear image of the intricate tapestry that is our future sustainability. Each thread, whether drawn from the realms of technology, ethics, or ecology, strengthens the weave of this fabric, inscribing within it our collective responsibility and the moral imperative to act.

Guided by the wisdom of historical conservation, fueled by the innovative drive spurring the renewable revolution, tempered by the understanding of our fragile biodiversity, and emboldened by the marriage of technological prowess and ecological wisdom, we can't help but envision a unified approach to sustaining our planet. The embodiment of our efforts, our successes tempered by setbacks, our systems united through synergy, and our technologies harnessed for good reflects the holistic view that sustainability isn't simply a goal but a continuous, co-creative journey.

It is within this framework we rest our hopes for a resilient, adaptive world, one not mired by denial or delay but empowered by proactive, fervent stewardship and a philosophical commitment to the health of all life on Earth. In this weave, our individual actions are interdependent, and each choice we make threads another line in the pattern of our collective future—a future we must endeavor to color with the most vibrant hues of sustainable practice.

Present Realities: Charting Successes and Setbacks

As we gaze upon the landscape of our current environmental efforts, we are met with a mixture of achievements and hindrances, like the interplay of shadow and light across the Earth's varied terrain. The task before us is not meager—it is an expansive, all-encompassing labor to co-create not simply a sustainable future but one that thrives on the resilience and adaptability of our systems and societies.

Successes emerge like blossoms in a long-withered field, demonstrating careful tending can lead to rejuvenation. Consider the advances in renewable energy uptake. Solar and wind power capacities have expanded at an unprecedented rate. The sharp decline in costs associated with these technologies has buoyed their deployment, encouraging a transition from fossil fuels to more planet-friendly alternatives.

Across the oceans, the establishment of Marine Protected Areas (MPAs) has offered a reprieve to beleaguered marine ecosystems. These sanctuaries have proven vital in preserving biodiversity, sustaining fish populations, and safeguarding Indigenous livelihoods tethered to the health of oceanic habitats.

Furthermore, in the realm of waste management, the concept of the circular economy is no longer just theoretical but is being implemented with increasing effectiveness. Cities and nations worldwide are enacting policies and systems that favor recycling, reuse, and reduction of waste. These efforts help close the loop on consumer goods, diminishing the strain on landfills and natural resources.

Yet, for every step forward, we seem to encounter barriers that require our collective ingenuity to overcome. Climate change continues to be an inexorable challenge with effects cascading across ecological, social, and economic domains. Even as renewable technologies advance, systemic inertia and vested interests in fossil fuels create headwinds against cleaner energy transitions.

Water scarcity remains a problem of dire proportions. As populations grow and climates shift, the need for innovative solutions to ensure water availability and purity has become a pressing concern, imposing significant health, economic, and social burdens on vulnerable communities worldwide.

Urban sprawl further taxes our water systems and infrastructures, often outpacing the planning and resources needed to maintain a sustainable water supply. These challenges are particularly acute in rapidly urbanizing regions of the developing world where infrastructure struggles to keep pace with growth.

Despite innovative strides in sustainable practices within agricultural arenas, conventional farming's grip remains steadfast, leaving a trail of degraded soils, biodiversity loss, and high greenhouse gas emissions. While the uptick in organic farming and agroforestry heralds a greener path, the transition is hampered by entrenched agricultural systems resistant to change.

Biodiversity continues to feel humanity's heavy hand. The extinction rates of species are accelerating, denuding the fabric of the biosphere and weakening the resilience of ecosystems vital for life support. Conservation efforts, although robust in some locales, are often fragmented and underfunded, struggling to stem the tide of loss.

These setbacks, however, cannot quell the human spirit's capacity for innovation and resilience. Communities worldwide are rising to the challenge, leveraging local knowledge and global science to craft solutions that are as diverse as the ecosystems they aim to protect. The quest for sustainability, faced with setbacks, drives the imperative for adaptive learning and the tenacious pursuit of solutions ever more deeply into our collective consciousness.

Appreciating these twin pillars of success and setbacks can inform our path forward. Recognizing advancements offers us a blueprint for action and an affirmation that we can accomplish monumental shifts. Acknowledging setbacks reminds us of the urgency and magnitude of the challenge—a challenge we must embrace with both humility and boldness.

It is vital that we do not lose sight of the intricate interconnectedness of our actions and their repercussions across the planet's systems. Each step toward sustainability tugs at a complex web of cause and effect, which underlines the need for integrated and holistic solutions.

In addressing these multifaceted challenges, we must be both fervent visionaries and grounded pragmatists. This dual focus allows us to hold tightly to our dreams of a sustainable world while navigating the thorny realities of the present. Fundamentally, sustainability requires us to be stewards not just of the environment but of hope—a hope that is continuously reborn with each act of conservation, each policy of protection, and each innovation for efficiency.

The present realities, encompassing both our successes and setbacks, offer us not just a reflection of where we stand, but also a map of where we need to go. As we chart our course, we must remain undaunted in the face of setbacks, learn and adapt as we go, and celebrate each success as evidence that a sustainable future is within reach if only we are bold enough to grasp it.

System Synergy: Interconnectedness and Holistic Solutions

In the labyrinthine challenge of sustainability, connections become pathways; the myriad parts of a system have indispensable roles that amass into a choir of ecological equipoise. This interlacing of elements demands a holistic approach in which water management, energy resources, waste reduction, and biodiversity conservation intersect, complementing each other rather than competing.

Understanding the interconnectedness of global systems is the key that turns the tide from piecemeal efforts to joint solutions. To exemplify, combining renewable energy projects with water conservation strategies aligns complementary sustainability goals. Reducing carbon emissions from clean energy sources can mitigate climate impact on water resources, illustrating this virtuous synergy. The holistic model is not just essential; it's inevitable for true sustainability.

Within this systemic synergy, the role of technology cannot be understated. Innovations in renewable energy can significantly abate the strain on freshwater resources, for energy production is invariably a thirsty process. By streamlining these technological advancements, societies can overcome conventional energy–water nexus hurdles.

Similarly, the circular economy paves the way to magnify the synergy between waste management and resource efficiency. By reimagining waste as a resource, the loop closes—reducing the need for new materials and the ecological burdens of raw material extraction and processing. This extends to agriculture, where organic waste can replenish soils and boost productivity in a cycle that honors the natural world.

The symbiotic relationship between land and sea further expounds the theme of interconnectedness. As climate change accelerates, the role of oceans as carbon sinks becomes increasingly vital, intersecting with terrestrial efforts to curb emissions. Thus, the protection of marine habitats supports atmospheric balance, showcasing the seamless ties across different ecological spheres.

Moreover, our oceanic endeavors reflect back onto land. Sustainable fishing practices safeguard marine biodiversity while ensuring the nutritional needs of millions are met without compromising future stocks. These practices must be woven together with agriculture strategies to form resilient food systems for a growing global population.

The holistic paradigm begs the inclusion of human communities, whose lifestyles and economic activities are parts of the intricate tapestry we seek to mend. Sustainability initiatives can flourish only when they embrace cultural diversity and harness community-based knowledge and leadership. Further, local needs and traditional wisdom can inspire universally applicable solutions.

For Indigenous communities, there's an inherent understanding of the interconnectedness of nature. Their practices, honed over millennia, often reflect sustainable management of resources and a profound respect for the connection between human and environmental health. Mainstream adoption and adaptation of traditional, nature-integrated practices can yield benefits surpassing the frontiers of those communities.

Education and empowerment further amplify system synergy. By equipping individuals and communities with knowledge and resources, the principles of sustainability can translate into actionable change. These stakeholders then become agents of sustainability, advocating for and implementing solutions that echo the ecosystems they rely on and inhabit.

Policymaking, too, needs to embrace the tenets of system synergy. Legislation that recognizes the co-dependence of energy, water, biodiversity, and waste systems can foster an environment conducive to integrated and sustainable management. Policies must be crafted to facilitate resource circulations, energy transitions, and protection of natural habitats in concert.

On a macro level, international cooperation bolsters this paradigm. Cross-border issues such as climate change, ocean governance, and migration linked to environmental catastrophes require joint solutions. Global treaties and collaborative projects underscore the reality that sustainability challenges—and their solutions—are inherently without borders.

Technology, when applied purposely and ethically, can serve as the connective tissue across these sustainability efforts. Smart grids for energy, water-sensitive urban design, and precision agriculture are examples of technological interfaces that can fortify interconnectedness among systems, sectors, and scales of operation.

At the nexus of system synergy lies resilience—the ability to withstand shocks and stresses. A holistic and interconnected approach to sustainability underscores the concept of resilience, as it builds the capacity of communities, economies, and ecosystems to adapt to and recover from disturbances, be they incremental or sudden.

Ultimately, embarking on the path of interconnectedness and holistic solutions in sustainability is a voyage toward equilibrium. It's a transition from viewing nature as a collection of discrete resources to seeing it as a comprehensive, living entity. This shift in perspective can't happen in isolation; it requires the collective will and concerted action of a myriad of humanity committed to the vitality of the Earth.

As we weave the threads of sustainability, the tapestry that emerges bears the hallmark of global guardianship. A world in which energy informs water policy, waste reduction benefits agriculture, and every action anticipates its ecological ripple effect is not merely idealistic; it's the framework for a sustainable and endurant civilization.

The Innovation Imperative: Technology's Role

In the quilt of measures weaving toward sustainability, technology's role emerges as critical—a kaleidoscope of innovation that can't be overstated. We stand at an unprecedented intersection in human history where technological prowess arms us with tools to sculpt our common future, one that can either be fraught with exacerbated inequalities and ecological ruin, or one in which harmony and prudence steer us toward a resilient planet, serving as the foundation for all life. The threads technology brings to this tapestry encompass renewable energy expansion, smart infrastructure, conservation technologies, precision agriculture, and beyond, each one vitally interwoven into the broad fabric of sustainable human progress.

The renewable energy revolution is one such thread directly spun from technological innovation. Advances in solar photovoltaics, wind turbines, battery storage, and smart grid technologies are vital to the unhinging of our energy systems from the vice grip of fossil fuels. But the impetus doesn't halt at energy production; the manner in which we consume and conserve power spins another enlightening tale.

Smart grids and AI-driven energy management systems exemplify how technology can optimize energy use, slash waste, and customize solutions to our living and workspaces. Buildings endowed with energy-efficient appliances, responsive lighting systems, and insulation advancements signify not only cost savings but a significant curtailment of our carbon footprints. These innovations aren't merely concepts; they're already proliferating within urban designs and future-thinking communities.

Conservation technology also unsheathes a mighty blade in our battle to preserve biodiversity. When we consider the multitude of species our world stands to lose, it's evident that advancements such as bioacoustic monitoring systems, wildlife tracking devices, and remote sensing technologies offer an unprecedented advantage in the conservation arena. They provide the necessary data to understand animal behaviors, habitat needs, and human–wildlife conflict areas, enabling informed conservation strategies.

The field of agriculture is similarly perched on the brink of a revolution, as technological advances promise solutions to the immense challenges of feeding a growing global population sustainably. Innovations in this sector range from genetically engineered crops that can withstand climate extremes to precision farming techniques that leverage GPS and IoT for optimized resource use. Drones that scout fields and software platforms that deliver real-time data to farmers embody a future in which every droplet of water and granule of fertilizer counts.

Furthermore, water, the very essence of life, is the focus of ingenious technological efforts. Desalination plants leveraging renewable energy, rainwater harvesting systems, and water purification technologies using nanomaterials and advanced membranes ensure clean and safe water isn't just a luxury but a viable reality for many facing water scarcity.

The fabric's pattern grows more complex when considering the vital intersection of technology with urban development. Here, smart cities emerge as potential cornerstones of sustainability. Through IoT, big data analytics, and clean transportation options, cities can transform into efficient, pollution-reducing, and livable spaces that promote not just sustainability, but also well-being.

Moving toward the high seas, advances in satellite tracking and automatic identification systems for vessels enable real-time monitoring of the oceans, thus, enhancing the management of marine protected areas and combating illegal fishing. Technologies enabling sustainable aquaculture practices promise to meet the growing demand for seafood while reducing the pressure on wild fish populations.

Yet, it's not all currents leading our ship toward favorable winds that we encounter on this journey. Challenges in technological equity and accessibility remain formidable barriers to the universal adoption of these innovations, especially in the rural and developing world contexts where infrastructure is sparse and investment scarce. The global digital divide, for instance, can render highly connected solutions ineffective where they might be most needed.

Recognizing these barriers demands not just innovation in the development of technologies, but also in their dissemination. Public–private partnerships, cross-border knowledge transfer, and scaling of low-cost, high-impact solutions are part of the multipronged approach needed to entrench technology in the heart of sustainable progress.

The march of technology also thrums with the beat of circular economies in which waste is transmuted into resource. Material science advancements make way for biodegradable plastics, recycling robotics fine-tune the reclamation of materials, and digital platforms elevate the reach and efficiency of sharing economies, collectively driving forward a paradigm where the life cycle of products aligns with the patterns of nature.

Thus, we can't neglect the cloth that binds it all together—education and access to information. Knowledge-sharing platforms, open-source technologies, and collaborative research databases act as looms, bringing together minds from disparate geographies and disciplines to foster innovations that leapfrog traditional barriers and accelerate sustainable development.

Conclusively, technology's role isn't simply supportive; it's transformative. As we weave the threads of sustainability, the innovations birthed today will define the landscapes of tomorrow. But it must be remembered that technology alone won't accomplish this herculean task. It operates hand in hand with the societal, economic, and political fabric, each needing to be equally robust and flexible. Technology, when properly aligned with global collaboration and equitable distribution, becomes not just an imperative for innovation, but also a beacon of hope for a planet teetering on the cusp of irreversible change.

As we envision the future, we see a world in which technology isn't a mere adjunct to sustainability; it is ingrained in the very essence of what we build, how we grow, and where we steer the shared fate of all Earthly inhabitants. It's upon us to craft this world with meticulous care, ensuring the quilt we create is one that shelters generations to come in its warm, life-sustaining embrace.

Unity in Action: Shared Responsibility

The threads of individual and collective action intertwine within the complexity of sustainability, yielding a fabric that is both resilient and expansive. The notion that we share the guardianship of our planet is not a new one, yet it is a message that demands not only understanding but bold action. The role of shared responsibility in realizing a sustainable future cannot be understated. Across every chapter of this book, the call for a collective approach to environmental challenges is clear, and it is within "Unity in Action" this call reverberates with particular clarity.

The concept of shared responsibility serves as a foundation for effective environmental governance. It suggests the actions of individuals, communities, organizations, and governments are indispensable threads in the overall fabric of sustainability. This cooperative approach is vital in a world where issues such as climate change, biodiversity loss, and pollution know no borders and are indifferent to political divides.

As we explore the multifaceted dimensions of sustainability, we witness a recurring theme: solutions must be inclusive and democratic. This is not the task of a few, but the duty of many. Shared responsibility means environmental scientists, students, policymakers, renewable energy professionals, activists, green economy entrepreneurs, and tech experts must all contribute their knowledge and abilities to this shared enterprise.

Equally essential is the participation of Indigenous communities. The Indigenous philosophy, which often encompasses an understanding of the interconnectedness of all life, offers a profound perspective on stewardship that complements modern scientific and technological approaches.

Shared responsibility also means recognizing the unequal burden climate change and environmental degradation impose on different populations. Vulnerable and marginalized communities often bear the brunt of environmental impacts despite contributing the least to the problem. Equity and justice must, therefore, be at the heart of sustainable initiatives, ensuring those with the least power but most at risk are included in decision making and benefit from sustainable development.

Businesses and the private sector have a significant role to play. Triple-bottom-line approaches that account for environmental and social performance alongside financial metrics exemplify how the business world can embody shared responsibility. Progressive companies are adopting sustainable practices not only to meet regulations, but also to innovate, reduce waste, conserve resources, and build long-term resilience.

For individuals, the notion of shared responsibility can manifest in everyday choices. Reducing energy consumption, choosing sustainable products, supporting eco-friendly businesses, and advocating for policies that protect the environment are all actions that contribute to the collective effort. Education and awareness raising among peers are additional ways individuals can expand the influence of environmental stewardship.

The role of policy and legislation in fostering shared responsibility is critical. Laws and regulations that support sustainable practices and hold polluters accountable are fundamental components of a society that values environmental integrity. Regulation alone, however, is insufficient; there must be a complementary emphasis on policies that incentivize innovation and reward sustainable advancements.

International cooperation, epitomized by agreements such as the Paris Climate Accord, underscores the global aspect of shared responsibility. Diplomatic efforts to reach a consensus on action against climate change exemplify how collective will transcends individual interests for the greater good. These frameworks, although challenging to negotiate, are pivotal in mounting a unified response to global environmental crises.

Education plays a pivotal role in cultivating a mindset geared toward shared responsibility. Through education, we can impart the skills and knowledge necessary to tackle complex environmental issues. Additionally, interdisciplinary approaches in education that integrate science, ethics, and policy create a more informed and proactive citizenry capable of engaging in nuanced environmental discourse.

The importance of integration of technology in advancing shared responsibility cannot be overstated. Innovations such as renewable energy, smart grids, and sustainable agriculture practices demonstrate how technological advancements can ally with environmental goals. These technologies must be accessible and equitable to ensure benefits are widely shared and not just limited to those with financial means or advanced infrastructures.

At the community level, shared responsibility takes shape through initiatives such as community gardens, local conservation efforts, and sustainability education programs. These localized actions, while seemingly small in isolation, collectively contribute to global sustainability by demonstrating the power of collective effort and fostering a sense of communal ownership over environmental outcomes.

Activism and advocacy are further embodiments of shared responsibility. Through movements that span the globe—ranging from youth-led climate strikes to community initiatives resisting environmental degradation—people are raising their voices to demand change. This activism helps to hold governments and corporations accountable while propelling environmental issues to the forefront of public consciousness.

In conclusion, shared responsibility is not merely a principle but a pragmatic strategy for enacting the changes necessary for sustainable living. It is an acknowledgment that the interwoven challenges we face require a matching complexity in our responses—a symphony of concerted actions that together forge a sustainable future. As we co-create tomorrow's sustainability, let us embrace our shared role with determination, creativity, and an unwavering commitment to the health of our planet and all its inhabitants.

Philosophies for Posterity: Ethics for the Anthropocene

As we weave together the multifaceted threads of sustainability, ethics remains a cornerstone. Our current epoch, characterized by massive human impact on the planet, necessitates an urgent revision of our ethical frameworks. In response, we spotlight the Anthropocene—a term signifying the current geological age of significant human influence—as a period demanding a redefined ethical stance toward our environment.

In this decisive era, we're confronted with the moral imperative to devise ethics that not only respect the biophysical limits of the Earth, but also promote justice within and between generations. It's imperative to consider a spectrum of values that honor both human and non-human entities in our shared biosphere. The intrinsic worth of ecosystems must be recognized, and their right to flourish uncontaminated by anthropogenic harms upheld.

Such ethical considerations align with theories of eco-centric morality in which nature's value is independent of human utility. Advocates argue sustainability initiatives must transcend economic calculus to recognize nature's inherent right to exist and evolve. As custodians of Earth, we have the responsibility to protect intricate life systems beyond short-term anthropocentric interests.

As thoughts of responsibility and stewardship are interwoven, notions of expanded environmental justice take center stage. This includes the consideration of vulnerable populations disproportionately affected by the effects of ecological degradation. Our ethical outlook in the Anthropocene must champion an equitable distribution of environmental benefits and burdens.

To embody these ethical approaches, movements such as Deep Ecology emphasize the interconnectedness of all biological entities. This philosophy asserts that a profound relational shift is necessary—one in which humanity sees itself as an integral part of the natural world rather than as dominate over it.

The continual advancement of technology in the Anthropocene propels discussions around ethics into new domains. Biotechnologies and geoengineering propose potential solutions to environmental issues, but also introduce complex ethical dilemmas. Our ethical frameworks must evolve to weigh potential benefits against risks of unforeseen consequences.

Moreover, the ethical approach to our planet's climate crisis cannot be sidelined. As nations negotiate reduction targets and strategies to mitigate climate change, a sense of global ethical solidarity is required. The imperative is clear: vulnerable nations and future generations depend on the choices we make today.

Our moral compass must also guide consumption patterns. A shift toward minimalism and conscious consumerism, underpinned by ethical deliberation on the impacts of our consumption choices, challenges the prevailing grow-or-die economic ideology. By embracing sustainability as a key ethical value, we can start to redefine success and wealth in terms of ecological health and societal well-being.

Education, too, plays a pivotal role in sculpting the ethical skeleton of the Anthropocene. From early education through to higher learning, embedding an appreciation for the natural world and an understanding of our impact on it is imperative. An education steeped in ecological ethics can foster responsible citizens who are both informed and empathetic toward environmental challenges.

Transitioning toward sustainable food systems calls for revising ethical standards in agriculture. Humane treatment of animals, responsible land use, and fair labor practices become central ethical considerations in promoting a food system that is both sustainable and just.

Through such a sweeping array of ethical considerations and reflective practices, the philosophical discourse of the Anthropocene seeks balance. It endeavors to harmonize the needs of present populations with those of future generations as well as human desires with the requirements of the non-human world.

Embedding ethics into the formulation of policies is another crucial juncture. Transparency, accountability, and participation stand as ethical cornerstones for policies that truly aspire to reach sustainable goals. The task is to translate ethical theory into norms and regulations that safeguard the vitality of ecosystems while fostering social equity.

Awareness of the Anthropocene compels us to question our anthropocentrism and embrace a more holistic environmental ethic. It's here sustainability finds its deepest roots—not in advancing green technologies or policies but in cultivating an empathetic and moral connection to all life forms with whom we share this extraordinary planet.

In conclusion, the tapestry of tomorrow's sustainability is rich and nuanced, composed of both tangible actions and intangible philosophical evolutions. Our legacy will be defined not only by the environmental milestones we achieve but by the ethical path we carve out as we journey toward them. The Anthropocene, as daunting as it may seem, offers an unparalleled opportunity for ethical growth and to co-create a world where sustainability and equity are not mere aspirations but lived realities.

Envisioning Unity: The Quest for Sustainable Futures

In the fertile ground of shared purpose and global urgency, the quest for a sustainable future stands as a monument to humanity's ability to adapt, innovate, and coalesce around common goals. As we traverse the tempest of environmental crises and societal challenges, envisioning unity becomes more than a lofty ideal; it's an essential strategy for survival and progress.

In reflecting on the chapters before, we recognize sustainability is not a destination but a dynamic journey. As we embark on this journey, we find the significance of intertwining disparate threads of thought, action, and discipline becomes increasingly apparent. We must harness the collective intellectual and emotional might of society to reimagine a world in which economic prosperity does not come at the expense of ecological health.

Envisioning unity in a sustainable future requires dismantling the silos that segregate expertise and hinder collaboration. Consider the farmer adapting age-old techniques to modern ecological challenges, or the policymaker drafting laws informed not only by economics but ecological sciences as well. Such unification is found in the cross-pollination of ideas and practices that transcend traditional boundaries.

The pursuit of a sustainable future is also about recognizing the intrinsic value of biodiversity and the services that ecosystems provide. In this tapestry of life, every thread—whether it is a microorganism or a megafauna—plays a crucial role. Unifying conservation efforts with economic incentives can create systems in which humans and nature flourish in harmony.

Addressing climate change, a challenge that sees no borders, epitomizes the need for global unity. The exchange of climate-smart practices and technologies globally, coupled with cooperative policy frameworks, exemplifies unity in action. It is an endeavor that warrants the active participation of every nation, every industry, and every individual.

With the increasing consciousness about the interdependencies between water, energy, and food security, cross-sectoral integration emerges as pivotal. This recognition can usher in a new era of collaboration in which water scarcity solutions support energy needs that, in turn, can bolster agricultural productivity in a cohesive loop.

As we navigate through the complexities of the marine commons, the unity of diverse stakeholders—fishers, scientists, policymakers, and community activists—remains paramount. Only through such unison can we effectively manage marine resources and safeguard the oceanic systems that regulate our planet's health.

The Ellen MacArthur Foundation's concept of a circular economy offers a roadmap for unity between economic activity and environmental integrity. This system rests on the pillars of reducing waste, reusing resources, and regenerating natural systems, establishing a sustainable cycle that benefits both development and the environment.

The charm of technological advancements lies in their potential to unify sustainable practice with everyday life. As emerging technologies provide solutions to age-old environmental problems, their widespread adoption hinges on building solidarity across all levels of society.

Innovations must be accessible and accountable to truly revolutionize our approach to sustainability.

Moreover, in agriculture, the combined knowledge of Indigenous practices and cutting-edge science heralds a new paradigm in food production. It combines cultural heritage and innovation to cultivate practices that can sustain the Earth and its inhabitants over the long term.

Unifying the goals of environmental conservation with economic development requires a deep understanding of human behavior and motivation. Strategies backed by behavioral science can lead the shift toward sustainable consumption patterns and foster a culture of stewardship.

The quest for a sustainable future reverberates with the need for educational reform that embeds sustainability into curricula worldwide. Enlightened by an educational focus on interdisciplinary learning, future generations can adapt to and overcome the intricacies of sustainability challenges.

As we edge closer to realizing this sustainable future, the dialogue must remain open, inclusive, and vibrant. Communities, once deemed too remote or marginalized to contribute, must be brought to the forefront of planning and implementation stages, adding unique perspectives and solutions to the global sustainability equation.

Ultimately, the unity that drives a sustainable future is fueled by an underlying ethics that treats the planet and its all inhabitants with respect and reverence. Acknowledging the rights of nature, as well as future human generations, embeds a moral compass that guides our steps toward genuine sustainability.

Envisioning unity within the pursuit of a sustainable future demands we rise to the challenge with open hearts and collaborative spirits. As we weave the threads of humanity's diverse experiences and wisdom, the tapestry of a sustainable world becomes possible. In this unity, there lies strength, resilience, and the hope for a thriving planet that sustains all forms of life for generations to come.

Glossary of Terms in *Our Changing World*

Throughout our conversation on *Our Changing World* and the multifaceted dimensions of sustainability, we've encountered a lexicon that is as varied as it is vital – a language shaping our understanding of not just where we stand, but also where we must go. This glossary serves as a compass to navigate the terrain of sustainability terms that appear throughout the book, ensuring clarity and fostering a deeper appreciation for the urgency and beauty in this journey toward a sustainable future.

Acculturation

Acculturation is a complex and multifaceted process where individuals or groups from one culture engage in continuous and direct interaction with another culture. This process leads to the adoption of new values, behaviors, and practices from the encountered culture.

Adaptation

The process through which individuals, communities, and ecosystems adjust to changes in their environment to mitigate harms or exploit beneficial opportunities. It is a cornerstone for resilience in the face of climate change, adjusting to its inevitable impacts.

Albedo

A measure of how much light that hits a surface is reflected without being absorbed. Surfaces with high albedo, such as ice and snow, can reflect more sunlight and affect climate by keeping temperatures cooler, whereas surfaces with low albedo, like forests or oceans, absorb more sunlight and can contribute to warming.

Animism

A belief system that posits that all objects, places, and creatures possess a distinct spiritual essence. In sustainability, this perspective can influence environmental policies and conservation efforts, emphasizing the intrinsic value of nature and the need to respect and preserve the spiritual integrity of the natural world.

Anthropocene

A proposed epoch marking the significant global impact of human activity on the Earth's geology and ecosystems, including climate change and biodiversity loss

Agroforestry

The practice of integrating trees and shrubs into crop and livestock farming systems to increase biodiversity, improve soil health, and enhance ecosystem services

Biodiversity

The variety within and among all species of plants, animals, and micro-organisms and the ecosystems of which they are part. This includes diversity within species, between species, and of ecosystems, forming the web of life of which humans are an integral part and upon which they fully depend.

Carbon Footprint

A measure of the total amount of greenhouse gases produced to directly and indirectly support human activities, typically expressed in equivalent tons of carbon dioxide (CO_2). Reducing our carbon footprint is key to combating climate change.

Circular Economy

An economic system aimed at minimizing waste and making the most of resources. This regenerative system aims to close the gap between production and natural ecosystem cycles—a stark contrast to the traditional linear economy, which has a 'take, make, dispose' model of production.

Climate Change
A long-term change in the average weather patterns that have come to define Earth's local, regional, and global climates. These changes have a broad range of observed effects that are synonymous with the term global warming.

Conservation
The protection, preservation, management, or restoration of natural environments and the ecological communities that inhabit them. Conservation is a means to ensure that nature will be around for future generations to enjoy and also recognizes the integral role nature plays in providing ecosystem services.

Corporate Social Responsibility (CSR)
A framework for businesses to voluntarily integrate social and environmental considerations into their operations and interactions with stakeholders. It's a commitment to manage the economic, social, and environmental impacts of a company's operations responsibly and in line with public expectations.

Cultural Capital
The collection of symbolic elements such as skills, tastes, posture, clothing, mannerisms, material belongings, and credentials that one acquires through being part of a particular social class.

Cultural Homogenization
The process by which local cultures are assimilated and eroded by dominant cultures, often as a result of globalization. This can lead to a loss of cultural diversity and the unique knowledge and practices that contribute to sustainability and resilience in various environmental contexts.

Cultural Sensitivity
Awareness and respect for cultural differences and the willingness to understand, communicate with, and effectively interact with people across cultures.

Cultural Sustainability

Maintaining and evolving cultural beliefs, practices, and heritage as part of a community's overall sustainability goals, with respect for diversity and tradition.

Cultural Tipping Points

Moments when a cultural norm or practice reaches a threshold and spreads rapidly, which can have significant implications for social sustainability.

Eco-Friendly Apparel

Clothing made from organic or recycled materials, using processes that minimize the environmental footprint during production, distribution, and disposal.

Eco-efficiency

Eco-efficiency is achieved by delivering competitively priced goods and services that satisfy human needs and bring quality of life, while progressively reducing ecological impacts and resource intensity throughout the life-cycle, to a level at least in line with the Earth's estimated carrying capacity.

Ecological Footprint

A measure of how much area of biologically productive land and water an individual, population, or activity requires to produce all the resources it consumes and to absorb the waste it generates.

Ecosystem Services

The many and varied benefits to humans that are provided by the natural environment and from healthy ecosystems. These include, but are not limited to, provisioning, regulating, cultural, and supporting services that directly or indirectly benefit human well-being.

Environmental, Social, and Governance (ESG)

Environmental, Social, and Governance (ESG) criteria are a set of standards for a company's operations that investors use to screen potential investments. Environmental criteria consider how a company safeguards the environment; social criteria examine how it manages relationships with employees, suppliers, customers, and communities; governance deals with a company's leadership, executive pay, audits, internal controls, and shareholder rights. ESG examines a company's non-financial materiality that may influence investor engagement.

Environmental Stewardship
The responsible management and care of the environment and natural resources with an emphasis on preserving and enhancing biodiversity and ecological integrity.

Epistemological Diversity
Recognition of the existence of multiple ways of knowing and understanding the world, which can be influenced by culture, language, and personal experience.

Ethical Consumerism
The practice of purchasing products and services that are produced ethically, considering the labor conditions, environmental impact, and animal welfare. Ethical consumerism encourages sustainable production practices and corporate social responsibility, influencing market trends toward more sustainable options.

Feedback Loop
A system where the output of a process is used as an input, leading to further output that may amplify (positive feedback) or diminish (negative feedback) the process.

Geopolitical Tensions
Political tensions influenced by geographic factors, often related to resource conflicts or environmental impacts.

Green Economics
An economic framework that takes into account ecological and social costs, promotes sustainability, and values the well-being of both the environment and society.

Grassroots Movements
Local, community-driven movements that grow to influence larger populations and policies, often associated with sustainability.

Holistic Thinking
An approach that considers the interconnectedness and complexity of systems, crucial for addressing sustainability challenges.

Indigenous Knowledge
Local knowledge unique to a culture, often contrasting with global knowledge systems and important for sustainability.

Indigenous Land Rights
The recognition of Indigenous peoples' rights to their traditional lands and resources, essential for cultural preservation and sustainable practices.

Interconnectedness
The recognition of the dependence of all life forms and ecosystems on each other, leading to an understanding that actions taken in one area can have global implications.

Intergenerational Equity
The concept of fairness or justice in relationships between the present and future generations, particularly in terms of resource allocation.

Isolationism
A policy or doctrine of isolating one's country from the affairs of other nations by declining to enter into alliances, foreign economic commitments, international agreements, etc., seeking to devote the entire efforts of one's country to its own advancement and remain at peace by avoiding foreign entanglements and responsibilities. In sustainability, isolationism can hinder global collaborative efforts needed to address worldwide environmental and social challenges.

Moral Imperatives
Principles or ethical considerations that compel individuals or societies to act in accordance with what is considered right and just.

Multicultural Curriculum
Educational syllabi that incorporate diverse cultural perspectives and content, thereby promoting inclusivity and understanding among students of different backgrounds.

Regenerative Design
Regenerative Design is a process-oriented approach to design. The goal is to develop systems that are capable of regenerating or restoring their own sources of energy and materials, thus creating sustainable patterns of consumption and production.

Renewable Energy
Energy from sources that are not depleted when used, such as wind or solar power, which are essential for sustainable development.

Resilience
The capacity of a system, community, or society potentially exposed to hazards to adapt, by resisting or changing in order to reach and maintain an acceptable level of functioning and structure. This is determined by the degree to which the social system is capable of organizing itself to increase its capacity for learning from past disasters for better future protection and to improve risk reduction measures.

Social Cohesion
The willingness of members of a society to cooperate with each other in order to survive and prosper, which can be essential for sustainable development.

Social Resilience
The ability of a community to withstand external shocks and stresses as a result of social capital and community resources.

Social Equity
The fair and just treatment of all individuals within society, ensuring equal access to opportunities and resources, and the protection from discrimination.

Societal Equilibrium
A state of balance in a society or ecosystem, where the social or natural structure is maintained over time, often through sustainable practices.

Socioeconomic Resilience
The ability of a social and economic system to recover from shocks and stresses, such as economic crises or natural disasters.

Sustainability
The ability to meet the needs of the present without compromising the ability of future generations to meet their own needs. Sustainability is often broken into three pillars: environmental, economic, and social, also known informally as planet, profit, and people.

Sustainable Agriculture
Farming that meets the needs of the present without compromising the ability of future generations to meet their own needs, typically involving environmentally friendly practices.

Sustainable Development
Development that meets the needs of the present without compromising the ability of future generations to meet their own needs, encompassing a balance between environmental, economic, and social goals.

Systems Thinking
A holistic approach to analysis that focuses on the way a system's parts interrelate and how systems work over time within the context of larger systems.

Tipping Point
A critical threshold at which a small change or influence can lead to a significant and often irreversible effect on a system. In sustainability, tipping points are crucial in the context of climate change and biodiversity, where they represent points beyond which systems may not recover, leading to drastic changes in the environment.

Traditional Ecological Knowledge (TEK)
A cumulative body of knowledge, practice, and belief, evolving by adaptive processes and handed down through generations by cultural transmission, about the relationship of living beings (including humans) with one another and with their environment.

Tragedy of the Commons
A situation in a shared-resource system where individual users acting independently according to their own self-interest behave contrary to the common good of all users by depleting or spoiling that resource through their collective action.

Zero-Carbon
Referring to an operation or activity that releases no carbon dioxide into the atmosphere. This ambitious goal can be approached by reducing emissions and implementing carbon offset schemes that compensate for any emissions that are produced. Zero-carbon is a guiding star in the journey toward climate neutrality.

References

Agardy, T., Bridgewater, P., Crosby, M. P., Day, J., Dayton, P. K., Kenchington, R., Laffoley, D., McConney, P., Murray, P. A., Parks, J. E., & Peau, L. (2003). Dangerous targets? Unresolved issues and ideological clashes around marine protected areas. Aquatic Conservation: Marine and Freshwater Ecosystems, 13(4), 353-367.

Altieri, M. A. (2004). Linking ecologists and traditional farmers in the search for sustainable agriculture. Frontiers in Ecology and the Environment, 2(1), 35-42.

Altieri, M. A., & Toledo, V. M. (2005). Natural Resource Management among Small-Scale Farmers in Semi-Arid Lands: Building on Traditional Knowledge and Agroecology. Annals of Arid Zone, 44(3&4), 365-385.

Bai, X., van der Heijden, J., Binz, C., McCormick, K., Luederitz, C., Olsson, G., ... & Yamagata, Y. (2018). Six research priorities for cities and climate change. Nature, 555(7694), 23-25.

Barbier, E. B., Hacker, S. D., Kennedy, C., Koch, E. W., Stier, A. C., & Silliman, B. R. (2011). The value of estuarine and coastal ecosystem services. Ecological Monographs, 81(2), 169-193.

Barnosky, A. D., Matzke, N., Tomiya, S., Wogan, G. O. U., Swartz, B., Quental, T. B., ... & Ferrer, E. A. (2011). Has the Earth's sixth mass extinction already arrived? Nature, 471(7336), 51-57.

Bengtsson, J., Ahnström, J., & Weibull, A.-C. (2005). The effects of organic agriculture on biodiversity and abundance: a meta-analysis. Journal of Applied Ecology, 42(2), 261-269.

Berkes, F., Colding, J., & Folke, C. (2000). Rediscovery of Traditional Ecological Knowledge as Adaptive Management. Ecological Applications, 10(5), 1251-1262.

Berry, T. (1988). The Dream of the Earth. Sierra Club Books.

Brashares, J. S., Golden, C. D., Weinbaum, K. Z., Barrett, C. B., & Okello, G. V. (2014). Economic and geographic drivers of wildlife consumption in rural Africa. Proceedings of the National Academy of Sciences, 111(34), 13964-13969.

Brouwer, C., Prins, K., Kay, M., & Heibloem, M. (1989). Irrigation Water Management: Irrigation Scheduling. Food and Agriculture Organization of the United Nations.

Brundtland Commission. (1987). Report of the World Commission on Environment and Development: Our Common Future. United Nations.

Bullock, D. G. (1992). Crop rotation. Critical Reviews in Plant Sciences, 11(4), 309-326.

Butchart, S. H., et al. (2010). Global biodiversity: Indicators of recent declines. Science, 328(5982), 1164-1168.

Cajete, G. (1999). Native Science: Natural Laws of Interdependence. Clear Light Publishers.

Ceballos, G., Ehrlich, P. R., Barnosky, A. D., García, A., Pringle, R. M., & Palmer, T. M. (2015). Accelerated modern human–induced species losses: Entering the sixth mass extinction. Science Advances, 1(5), e1400253.

Clark, R. B. (2001). Marine pollution. Oxford University Press.

Commission of the European Communities. (2000). Communication from the Commission on the precautionary principle.

Cortese, A. D. (2003). The critical role of higher education in creating a sustainable future. Planning for higher education, 31(3), 15-22.

Costanza, R., d'Arge, R., de Groot, R., Farber, S., Grasso, M., Hannon, B., ... & van den Belt, M. (1997). The value of the world's ecosystem services and natural capital. Nature, 387(6630), 253-260.

Creutzig, F., Agoston, P., Goldschmidt, J. C., Luderer, G., Nemet, G., & Pietzcker, R. C. (2017). The underestimated potential of solar energy to mitigate climate change. Nature Energy, 2(9), 17140. https://doi.org/10.1038/nenergy.2017.140

Crowder, D. W., & Reganold, J. P. (2015). Financial competitiveness of organic agriculture on a global scale. Proceedings of the National Academy of Sciences, 112(24), 7611-7616.

Daily, G. C. (Ed.). (1997). Nature's services: Societal dependence on natural ecosystems. Island Press.

Daily, G. C., Polasky, S., Goldstein, J., Kareiva, P. M., Mooney, H. A., Pejchar, L., ... Shallenberger, R. (2009). Ecosystem services in decision making: time to deliver. Frontiers in Ecology and the Environment, 7(1), 21-28. doi:10.1890/080025

Daly, H. E., & Farley, J. (2011). Ecological Economics: Principles and Applications. Island Press.

Davis, A. S., Hill, J. D., Chase, C. A., Johanns, A. M., & Liebman, M. (2012). Increasing cropping system diversity balances productivity, profitability and environmental health. PLoS ONE, 7(10), e47149.

Demeter International. (n.d.). Certified Biodynamic(R) Criteria. Retrieved from https://www.demeter.net/certification/criteria

Derpsch, R., Friedrich, T., Kassam, A., & Li, H. (2010). Current status of adoption of no-till farming in the world and some of its main benefits. International Journal of Agricultural and Biological Engineering, 3(1), 1-25.

Díaz, S., Settele, J., Brondízio, E. S., Ngo, H. T., Guèze, M., Agard, J., ... & Zayas, C. N. (2019). Pervasive human-driven decline of life on Earth points to the need for transformative change. Science, 366(6471).

Dirzo, R., Young, H. S., Galetti, M., Ceballos, G., Isaac, N. J. B., & Collen, B. (2014). Defaunation in the Anthropocene. Science, 345(6195), 401-406.

Ebi, K. L., Woodruff, R., von Hildebrand, A., & Corvalan, C. (2006). Climate change-related health impacts in the Hindu Kush-Himalayas. EcoHealth, 3(3), 264-270.

Edgar, G. J., Stuart-Smith, R. D., Willis, T. J., Kininmonth, S., Baker, S. C., Banks, S., ... & Thomson, R. J. (2014). Global conservation outcomes depend on marine protected areas with five key features. Nature, 506(7487), 216-220.

Elimelech, M., & Phillip, W. A. (2011). The future of seawater desalination: Energy, technology, and the environment. Science, 333(6043), 712–717. https://doi.org/10.1126/science.1200488

Elkington, J. (1997). Cannibals with Forks: The Triple Bottom Line of 21st Century Business. New Society Publishers.

Fernandez-Gimenez, M. E., & Fillat Estaque, F. (2012). Pyrenean pastoralists' ecological knowledge: Documentation and application to natural resource management and adaptation. Human Ecology, 40(2), 287-300.

Field, C. B., Behrenfeld, M. J., Randerson, J. T., & Falkowski, P. (1998). Primary production of the biosphere: integrating terrestrial and oceanic components. Science, 281(5374), 237-240.

Fischhoff, B., & Davis, A. L. (2014). Communicating scientific uncertainty. Proceedings of the National Academy of Sciences, 111(Supplement 4), 13664-13671.

Folke, C., Holling, C. S. & Perrings, C. (2005). Biodiversity and Ecosystem Services: A Multiscale Empirical Study of the Relationship Between Species Richness and Net Primary Production. Ecological Economics, 41(3), 369-392.

Ghisellini, P., Cialani, C., & Ulgiati, S. (2016). A review on circular economy: the expected transition to a balanced interplay of environmental and economic systems. Journal of Cleaner Production, 114, 11-32.

Gibbs, L. M. (1982). Love Canal: My Story. State University of New York Press.

Giddings, B., Hopwood, B., & O'Brien, G. (2002). Environment, economy and society: Fitting them together into sustainable development. Sustainable Development, 10(4), 187-196.

Gleick, P. H. (2000). The World's Water 2000-2001: The Biennial Report on Freshwater Resources. Island Press.

Goodall, J. (1990). Through a Window: My Thirty Years with the Chimpanzees of Gombe. Houghton Mifflin Company.

Gottlieb, R. (2005). Forcing the spring: The transformation of the American environmental movement. Island Press.

Govan, H., Aalbersberg, W., Tawake, A., & Parks, J. (2008). Locally-Managed Marine Areas: A guide for practitioners. The Locally-Managed Marine Area (LMMA) Network.

Grant, K., Goldizen, F. C., Sly, P. D., Brune, M. N., Neira, M., van den Berg, M., & Norman, R. E. (2013). Health consequences of exposure to e-waste: A systematic review. The Lancet Global Health, 1(6), e350-e361.

Gustavsson, J., Cederberg, C., Sonesson, U., van Otterdijk, R., & Meybeck, A. (2011). Global Food Losses and Food Waste. FAO.

Halpern, B. S. (2003). The impact of marine reserves: do reserves work and does reserve size matter? Ecological Applications, 13(sp1), 117-137.

Hamilton, L. (2020). Understanding the complexities of climate change: A foundational guide for decision-makers. Global Environmental Strategies, 57(1), 65-79. doi:10.1177/0078722920917765

Heller, N. E., & Zavaleta, E. S. (2009). Biodiversity management in the face of climate change: A review of 22 years of recommendations. Biological Conservation, 142(1), 14-32.

Henry, L. (2017). Health care in remote communities: Challenges and solutions. Journal of Community Health, 42(2), 422-428.

Hernandez, P., Kenny, P., & Fromer, N. (2014). Design and analysis of a net-zero energy commercial office building in a hot and humid climate. Applied Energy, 114, 512-523.

Homewood, K. (1992). Development and the ecology of Maasai food and nutrition. Ecology of Food and Nutrition, 29(1), 61-80.

Hopkins, R., & Roberts, D. (2021). Urban Sustainability and Resilience: The Role of Technology. Smart Cities, 4(2), 423-435.

Hutton, G. (2012). Global costs and benefits of drinking-water supply and sanitation interventions to reach the MDG target and universal coverage. WHO.

Hynes, H. P. (1989). The Recurring Silent Spring. Pergamon Press.

International Energy Agency. (2020). Sustainable Recovery. https://www.iea.org

IRENA. (2020). Renewable Capacity Statistics 2020. International Renewable Energy Agency.

Johnson, E., & Brown, K. (2020). Sustainable Development: Bridging the Research and Policy Gap. International Journal of Environmental Research and Public Health, 17(2), 432. https://doi.org/10.3390/ijerph17020432

Junk, W. J., An, S., Finlayson, C. M., Gopal, B., Květ, J., Mitchell, S. A., ... & Xiao, X. (2013). Current state of knowledge regarding the world's wetlands and their future under global climate change: a synthesis. Aquatic Sciences, 75(1), 151-167.

Kaspar, T. C., & Singer, J. W. (2011). The use of cover crops to manage soil. Soil management: building a stable base for agriculture, 321-337.

Kassam, A., Friedrich, T., Shaxson, F., & Pretty, J. (2019). The spread of Conservation Agriculture: Justification, sustainability and uptake. International Journal of Agricultural Sustainability, 7(4), 292-320.

Keesing, F., Belden, L. K., Daszak, P., Dobson, A., Harvell, C. D., Holt, R. D., ... & Ostfeld, R. S. (2010). Impacts of biodiversity on the emergence and transmission of infectious diseases. Nature, 468(7324), 647-652.

Keith, D. W., Parson, E., & Morgan, M. G. (2010). Research on global sun block needed now. Nature, 463(7280), 426-427.

Kempton, W., Tomić, J., Letendre, S., Brooks, A., & Lipman, T. (2008). Vehicle-to-grid power: Battery, hybrid, and fuel cell vehicles as resources for distributed electric power in California. UC Davis: Institute of Transportation Studies.

Khan, S., Shahid, M., Hedberg, Y. S., White, J. C., & Khan, M. H. (2016). Waste management and human health: A case study in the Lahore metropolitan of Pakistan. Environmental Science and Pollution Research, 23(20), 20996-21008.

Kirchherr, J., Reike, D., & Hekkert, M. (2017). Conceptualizing the circular economy: An analysis of 114 definitions. Resources, Conservation and Recycling, 127, 221-232.

Klein, N. (2014). This changes everything: Capitalism vs. The climate. Simon & Schuster.

Korhonen, J., Nuur, C., Feldmann, A., & Birkie, S. E. (2018). Circular economy as an essentially contested concept. Journal of Cleaner Production, 175, 544-552.

Krause, R. M. (2011). Policy innovation, intergovernmental relations, and the adoption of climate protection initiatives by U.S. cities. Journal of Urban Affairs, 33(1), 45-60.

Kurucz, E. C., Colbert, B. A., & Wheeler, D. (2014). Reconstructing value: Leadership skills for a sustainable world. University of Toronto Press.

Lancaster, B. (2006). Rainwater Harvesting for Drylands and Beyond, Volume 1: Guiding Principles to Welcome Rain into Your Life and Landscape. Rainsource Press.

Lee, M., Tansel, B., & Balbin, M. (2018). Advances in water purification techniques: Meeting the needs of developed and developing countries. Sustainable Water Resources Management, 4(4), 793-807.

Leopold, A. (1949). A Sand County Almanac, And Sketches Here And There. Oxford University Press.

Likens, G. E. (1992). The Ecosystem Approach: Its Use and Abuse. Ecology Institute.

Lipper, L., Thornton, P., Campbell, B. M., Baedeker, T., Braimoh, A., Bwalya, M., ... & Torquebiau, E. F. (2014). Climate-smart agriculture for food security. Nature Climate Change, 4(12), 1068.

Lowenberg-DeBoer, J., & Erickson, B. (2019). Setting the Record Straight on Precision Agriculture Adoption. Agronomy Journal, 111(4), 1552-1569.

Lubchenco, J. (1998). Entering the Century of the Environment: A New Social Contract for Science. Science, 279(5350), 491-497.

Lytle, M. H. (2007). The gentle subversive: Rachel Carson, Silent Spring, and the rise of the environmental movement. Oxford University Press.

Manzini, E., & Vezzoli, C. (2003). A strategic design approach to develop sustainable product service systems: Examples taken from the 'environmentally friendly innovation' Italian prize. Journal of Cleaner Production, 11(8), 851-857.

Marin, A., & Berkes, F. (2013). Local people's responses to coastal erosion in Tuktoyaktuk, Northwest Territories, Canada. Environmental Management, 51(4), 923-938.

Marsh, G. P. (1864). Man and Nature; or, Physical Geography as Modified by Human Action. Charles Scribner.

Mekonnen, M. M., & Hoekstra, A. Y. (2016). Four billion people facing severe water scarcity. Science Advances, 2(2), e1500323.

Millennium Ecosystem Assessment (MEA). (2005). Ecosystems and Human Well-being: Synthesis. Island Press.

Miller, G. T., & Spoolman, S. E. (2012). Living in the Environment. Brooks/Cole.

Milly, P. C. D., Betancourt, J., Falkenmark, M., Hirsch, R. M., Kundzewicz, Z. W., Lettenmaier, D. P., & Stouffer, R. J. (2008). Stationarity is dead: Whither water management? Science, 319(5863), 573-574.

Mollison, B., & Holmgren, D. (1978). Permaculture One: A Perennial Agriculture for Human Settlements. Transworld Publishers.

Morton, C., Aw-Hassan, A., & Almekhlafi, F. A. (2016). Water Harvesting and Soil Moisture Retention. In Water-Smart Agriculture in East Africa (pp. 246-252). ICRAF.

Murphy, P. (2005). What a book can do: The publication and reception of Silent Spring. University of Massachusetts Press.

Musial, W., & Ram, B. (2010). Large-Scale Offshore Wind Power in the United States: Assessment of Opportunities and Barriers. U.S. Department of Energy, Energy Efficiency and Renewable Energy (EERE).

Naess, A. (1973). The shallow and the deep, long-range ecology movement. Inquiry, 16(1-4), 95-100.

Naess, A. (1973). The shallow and the deep, long-range ecology movement. A summary. Inquiry, 16(1-4), 95-100.

Nash, R. (2001). Wilderness and the American Mind. Yale University Press.

Nash, R. (2014). Wilderness and the American mind. Yale University Press.

National Environmental Policy Act of 1969, Pub. L. 91-190, 42 U.S.C. § 4321-4347 (1970).

Newell, P., & Paterson, M. (2010). Climate capitalism: Global warming and the transformation of the global economy. Cambridge University Press.

Novacek, M. J. (2008). Engaging the public in biodiversity issues. Proceedings of the National Academy of Sciences, 105(Supplement 1), 11571-11578.

O'Neill, K. & Hultman, N. (2019). Bridging the sustainability gap: Policy and practice for the new environmental reality. Nature Sustainability, 2(4), 343-349. doi:10.1038/s41893-019-0273-7

Odum, E. P. (1963). Ecology. Holt, Rinehart and Winston.

Onda, K., LoBuglio, J., & Bartram, J. (2012). Global access to safe water: accounting for water quality and the resulting impact on MDG progress. International journal of environmental research and public health, 9(3), 880-894.

Oreskes, N., & Conway, E. M. (2010). Merchants of Doubt. Bloomsbury Press.

Orr, D. W. (1992). Ecological literacy: Education and the transition to a postmodern world. SUNY Press.

Orr, D. W. (2002). Four Challenges of Sustainability. Conservation Biology, 16(6), 1457-1460.

Orr, D. W. (2006). The nature of design: ecology, culture, and human intention. Oxford University Press.

Orr, J.C., Fabry, V.J., Aumont, O., Bopp, L., Doney, S.C., Feely, R.A., ... & Yool, A. (2005). Anthropogenic ocean acidification over the twenty-first century and its impact on calcifying organisms. Nature, 437(7059), 681-686.

Parsa, S., Morse, S., Bonifacio, A., Chancellor, T. C. B., Condori, B., Crespo-Pérez, V., ... & Quiróz, R. (2014). Obstacles to integrated pest management adoption in developing countries. Proceedings of the National Academy of Sciences, 111(10), 3889-3894.

Pauly, D., & Zeller, D. (2016). Catch reconstructions reveal that global marine fisheries catches are higher than reported and declining. Nature communications, 7, 10244.

Pimentel, D., et al. (2005). Environmental, energetic, and economic comparisons of organic and conventional farming systems. BioScience, 55(7), 573-582.

Pinchot, G. (1910). The Fight for Conservation. Doubleday, Page & Company.

Poeplau, C., & Don, A. (2015). Carbon sequestration in agricultural soils via cultivation of cover crops – A meta-analysis. Agriculture, Ecosystems & Environment, 200, 33-41.

Prendeville, S., Cherim, E., & Bocken, N. (2018). Circular cities: Mapping six city case studies worldwide. Procedia CIRP, 69, 824-830.

Pretty, J., & Bharucha, Z. P. (2014). Sustainable intensification in agricultural systems. Annals of Botany, 114(8), 1571-1596.

Radkau, J. (2008). Nature and Power: A Global History of the Environment. Cambridge University Press.

Redford, K. H. (1992). The Empty Forest. BioScience, 42(6), 412-422.

Reich, P. B. (2012). Key concepts and terminology of ecology. In Leemans, R. (Ed.), Ecological Systems: Selected Entries from the Encyclopedia of Sustainability Science and Technology (pp. 1-24). Springer.

Revkin, A. C. (2004). The Burning Season: The Murder of Chico Mendes and the Fight for the Amazon Rain Forest. Island Press.

Richerson, P. J., & Boyd, R. (2005). Not by genes alone: How culture transformed human evolution. University of Chicago Press.

Roberts, J. T., & Parks, B. C. (2019). A Climate of Injustice: Global Inequality, North-South Politics, and Climate Policy. MIT Press.

Rosenzweig, C., Solecki, W., Hammer, S. A., & Mehrotra, S. (2011). Climate change and cities: First assessment report of the Urban Climate Change Research Network. Cambridge University Press.

Rothausen, S. G. S. A., & Conway, D. (2011). Greenhouse-gas emissions from energy use in the water sector. Nature Climate Change, 1(4), 210–219. https://doi.org/10.1038/nclimate1147

Ruiz, M., & Ruiz, J. P. (1986). Ecological history of transhumance in Spain. Biological Conservation, 37(1), 73-86.

Sachs, J. D., Schmidt-Traub, G., Kroll, C., Lafortune, G., & Fuller, G. (2019). Sustainable Development Report 2019. Bertelsmann Stiftung and Sustainable Development Solutions Network (SDSN).

Sanjayan, M. A., Schill, S. R., & Zulueta, R. C. (2016). Connecting Nature, Connecting People. Can Green Infrastructure Serve as a Foundation for Sustainable Conservation? In A. Aguirre, R. Sukumar (Eds.), Tropical Conservation: Perspectives on Local and Global Priorities (pp. 261-273). Oxford University Press.

Schelly, C. (2014). Implementing renewable energy portfolio standards: The good, the bad, and the ugly in a two state comparison. Energy Policy, 67, 543-551.

Schlenker, W., & Roberts, M. J. (2009). Nonlinear temperature effects indicate severe damages to U.S. crop yields under climate change. Proceedings of the National Academy of Sciences, 106(37), 15594-15598.

Seddon, N., Mace, G. M., Naeem, S., Tobias, J. A., Pigot, A. L., Cavanagh, R., ... & Alkemade, R. (2016). Biodiversity in the Anthropocene: prospects and policy. Proceedings of the Royal Society B: Biological Sciences, 283(1844), 20162094.

Shepherd, J., Caldeira, K., Cox, P., Haigh, J., Keith, D., Launder, B., ... & Shaffer, G. (2009). Geoengineering the climate: science, governance and uncertainty. The Royal Society.

Shiva, V. (1988). Staying Alive: Women, Ecology and Development. Zed Books.

Shiva, V. (2010). Stolen Harvest: The Hijacking of the Global Food Supply. South End Press.

Slovic, P. (1993). Perceived Risk, Trust, and Democracy. Risk Analysis, 13(6), 675-682.

Smith, A., & Harrington, J. (2017). Sustainable agriculture - historical perspective and future outlook. Journal of Sustainable Agriculture, 2(3), 1-15.

Smith, J., & Wang, L. (2019). Infrastructure for Sustainable Water Resources Management: The Role of Technology and Governance. Water Resources Management, 33(15), 4755-4771.

Smith, J., Liu, Z., & Carlton, S. J. (2021). Climate change action: the goals and mechanisms for a sustainable future. Environmental Progress & Sustainable Energy, 40(1), e13422.

Smith, T., Jones, B., & Roberts, L. (2019). Environmental Impact of Space Flight: Challenges and Opportunities. Advances in Space Research, 63(8), 2490-2496.

Snapp, S. S., Swinton, S. M., Labarta, R., Mutch, D., Black, J. R., Leep, R., ... & O'Neil, K. (2005). Evaluating cover crops for benefits, costs and performance within cropping system niches. Agronomy Journal, 97(1), 322-332.

Steenweg, R., Hebblewhite, M., Kays, R., Ahumada, J., Fisher, J. T., Burton, C., ... & Rich, L. N. (2017). Scaling-up camera traps: monitoring the planet's biodiversity with networks of remote sensors. Frontiers in Ecology and the Environment, 15(1), 26-34.

Steffen, W., Broadgate, W., Deutsch, L., Gaffney, O., & Ludwig, C. (2015). The trajectory of the Anthropocene: The Great Acceleration. The Anthropocene Review, 2(1), 81-98.

Stern, N. (2006). The Economics of Climate Change: The Stern Review. Cambridge University Press.

Stern, N., Stern, P., & Stern, J. (2016). Economics of Climate Change. American Economic Review, 98(2), 1-37.

Takeuchi, K. (Ed.). (2010). Satoyama: The Traditional Rural Landscape of Japan. Springer Science & Business Media.

Thapa, G. B. (2019). Organic farming practice in Nepal: a review of challenges and opportunities. Agriculture & Food Security, 8(1).

Thompson, A., Ruckelshaus, M., & Flanders, N. R. (2023). Engaging the public with climate change through environmental storytelling and behavioral sciences. Environmental Communication, 17(2), 301-316.

Thompson, R. C., Swan, S. H., Moore, C. J., & vom Saal, F. S. (2009). Our plastic age. Philosophical Transactions of the Royal Society B: Biological Sciences, 364(1526), 1973-1976.

Thoreau, H. D. (1854). Walden; or, Life in the Woods. Ticknor and Fields.

Tilman, D., & Clark, M. (2014). Global diets link environmental sustainability and human health. Nature, 515(7528), 518-522.

UNFCCC. (2015). Paris Agreement. United Nations Framework Convention on Climate Change. Retrieved from http://unfccc.int/resource/docs/2015/cop21/eng/l09r01.pdf

United Nations Environment Programme. (1972). Declaration of the United Nations Conference on the Human Environment. UNEP.

United Nations World Water Assessment Programme. (2021). The United Nations World Water Development Report 2021: Valuing Water. UNESCO.

United Nations. (2010). The human right to water and sanitation. UN General Assembly, 64/292.

United Nations. (2015). Paris Agreement. United Nations Framework Convention on Climate Change.

United Nations. (2015). Transforming our world: the 2030 Agenda for Sustainable Development. Retrieved from https://sustainabledevelopment.un.org/post2015/transformingourworld

Waas, T., Verbruggen, A., & Wright, T. (2011). University research for sustainable development: Definition and characteristics explored. Journal of Cleaner Production, 18(7), 629-636.

Wackernagel, M., & Rees, W. (1998). Our ecological footprint: Reducing human impact on the earth. New Society Publishers.

Walker, T. (2022). Ethics for the Anthropocene: Navigating the Future of Sustainability. Ecological Economics, 190, 107141. https://doi.org/10.1016/j.ecolecon.2021.107141

Wals, A. E., & Jickling, B. (2002). "Sustainability" in higher education: From doublethink and newspeak to critical thinking and meaningful learning. International Journal of Sustainability in Higher Education, 3(3), 221-232.

Washington, H. (2015). Demystifying Sustainability: Towards Real Solutions. Routledge.

Webster, K. (2017). The Circular Economy: A Wealth of Flows. London: Ellen MacArthur Foundation Publishing.

White, R. (2011). The organic machine: The remaking of the Columbia River. Hill and Wang.

Wilcove, D. S., Rothstein, D., Dubow, J., Phillips, A., & Losos, E. (1998). Quantifying threats to imperiled species in the United States. BioScience, 48(8), 607-615.

Wilkinson, R. & Pickett, K. (2017). The case for greening the economy: Ecological and social arguments for change. Ecological Economics Review, 132, 4-14. doi:10.1016/j.ecolecon.2017.01.002

Willey, R. W. (1990). Resource use in intercropping systems. Agricultural Water Management, 17(1-3), 215-231.

Williams, E., & Ayres, R. U. (2023). The material and energy intensity of new technologies. Journal of Industrial Ecology, 27(1), 236-250.

Wilson, E. O. (2016). Half-Earth: Our Planet's Fight for Life. Liveright Publishing.

WWAP (United Nations World Water Assessment Programme). (2019). The United Nations World Water Development Report 2019: Leaving No One Behind. UNESCO.

Xu, J., & Grumbine, R. E. (2014). Integrating local hybrid knowledge and state support for climate change adaptation in the Asian Highlands. Climatic Change, 124(1-2), 93-104.

Zhang, C., & Kovacs, J. M. (2012). The application of small unmanned aerial systems for precision agriculture: a review. Precision Agriculture, 13(6), 693–712. https://doi.org/10.1007/s11119-012-9274-5